What Happens Next?

1-7-13 Many thanks to Rick Schostek, my neighbor, for sharing his book with me. Rick does an outstanding job of sharing real feelings and obstacles in raising a child with ASD. His honesty, openness and wisdom are amazing. I knew Greg as a toddler and am so proud to hear about his accomplishments in life so far. Patti Johnson

1-22-13 Many thanks to Patti Johnson, my dear friend and coworker, who passed this book on to me. Rick's book ~~was~~ is honest and heartfelt. I could relate to many of his situations after taking care of and then watching my nephew grow up with ASD. Thanks for sharing your story, Rick.

What Happens Next?

Raising a Son with Autism: A Father's Story

by Rick Schostek

What Happens Next?
Raising a Son with Autism: A Father's Story
By Rick Schostek

Library of Congress Control Number: 2011938410

ISBN 978-1-4507-9299-8

Printed in the United States of America

Book design by o2ideas, Inc.

Please visit www.whathappensnextbook.com

To Greg, my hero.

Forward

Our son Greg loves *Sesame Street.* The show's characters are practically a part of our family. Greg has memorized countless skits and songs. He knows more Spanish words than his parents do, thanks to Luis, Maria, Rosita and the other characters on the show.

Sesame Street's lessons and lyrics are quite helpful for us. A couple of times a month, in response to a spilled drink or a wrong turn, Greg or I will cite Big Bird's tuneful advice: "Everyone Makes Mistakes." Greg sometimes counts in the manner of Count von Count, adding "ah ah ah" when he's finished.

I'm sure there are many families who benefit from the teachings of the Children's Television Workshop. I'm equally sure that our family is somewhat unique in our connection to *Sesame Street.*

Greg is 23 years old.

Contents

Part 1

Introduction

Welcome to the world of autism,
where normal is a button on the clothes dryer.

Chapter 1: Changing Trains

Greg has autism. In today's terms, he's "on the spectrum." He's one of millions of people who live with Autism Spectrum Disorder, or ASD. The incidence rate of ASD has increased dramatically throughout Greg's lifetime. In the early 1990s, when he was diagnosed, the rate was 15 in 10,000. Now it's 1 in 110. In other words, now six times more common.

No one knows why. Better awareness and diagnostic tools account for some of the increase. That means cases of autism were either not being diagnosed or were being categorized differently 20 years ago. That doesn't explain the entire increase. Something else is going on.

Recently, ASD has received a lot of media attention, attributed to the increased incidence rate and the mysteries of the disorder. Autism occurs everywhere in the population, across all races, ethnicities and socioeconomic backgrounds. Many celebrities have a child with ASD in their family and are willing to share their experiences. Football players and coaches like Dan Marino, Doug

Flutie, Rodney Peete and Charlie Weiss. Golfer Ernie Els. Entertainers like Sly Stallone, Jenny McCarthy and Toni Braxton. NASCAR drivers Jamie McMurray and Elliot Sadler each have a niece with autism, and the Autism Speaks 400 is a regular race in the Sprint Cup series.

This is all good. It's meant more awareness, earlier diagnoses and increased research funding. The media attention is, however, 99 percent focused on children with autism.

Greg isn't the first young man or woman with ASD to transition to adulthood. With the increased incidence rate, he and others are at the leading edge of a wave of adults with ASD. In the last decade, our school systems faced a huge challenge with this growing population. Is our adult services infrastructure now ready for this wave?

When Greg was a young boy, I read an essay entitled *Welcome to Holland*. An excellent life perspective from a parent of a child with special needs. When we began to focus on Greg's transition to adulthood, I set out to find and re-read the essay. I learned it was written by Emily Perl Kingsley, the mother of a child with Down Syndrome and a writer for *Sesame Street* since 1970! What's more, she wrote the essay in 1987, the year Greg was born. Too much coincidence - her essay must have been meant for us:

Welcome to Holland

By Emily Perl Kingsley

I am often asked to describe the experience of raising a child with a disability - to try to help people who have not shared that unique experience to understand it, to imagine how it would feel. It's like this......

When you're going to have a baby, it's like planning a fabulous vacation trip - to Italy. You buy a bunch of guide books and make your wonderful plans. The Coliseum. The Michelangelo David. The gondolas in Venice. You may learn some handy phrases in Italian. It's all very exciting.

After months of eager anticipation, the day finally arrives. You pack your bags and off you go. Several hours later, the plane lands. The stewardess comes in and says, "Welcome to Holland."

"Holland?!?" you say. "What do you mean Holland?? I signed up for Italy! I'm supposed to be in Italy. All my life I've dreamed of going to Italy."

But there's been a change in the flight plan. They've landed in Holland and there you must stay.

The important thing is that they haven't taken you to a horrible, disgusting, filthy place, full of pestilence, famine and disease. It's just a different place.

So you must go out and buy new guide books. And you must learn a whole new language. And you will meet a whole new group of people you would never have met.

It's just a different place. It's slower-paced than Italy, less flashy than Italy. But after you've been there for a while and you catch your breath, you look around.... and you

> *begin to notice that Holland has windmills....and Holland has tulips. Holland even has Rembrandts.*
>
> *But everyone you know is busy coming and going from Italy... and they're all bragging about what a wonderful time they had there. And for the rest of your life, you will say "Yes, that's where I was supposed to go. That's what I had planned."*
>
> *And the pain of that will never, ever, ever, ever go away... because the loss of that dream is a very very significant loss.*
>
> *But... if you spend your life mourning the fact that you didn't get to Italy, you may never be free to enjoy the very special, the very lovely things ... about Holland.*

Ms. Kingsley got it right. The journey we've taken with Greg these last 23 years has been frustrating and adventurous, difficult and rewarding. We've been navigating our way around Holland for a long time. We're familiar with the important train routes.

In the United States, the age of 22 is when a train track runs out for people with disabilities. The federal education law promises a free and appropriate public education to children with disabilities – until the age of 22. That's when service entitlement ends. There are programs and services for adults, but they lack the predictability and stability of school programs. Adults with disabilities aren't entitled to services. The system is based on eligibility and availability. Circumstances can change quickly. Vocational and housing arrangements can dissolve overnight.

Greg has come to the end of that line. Dropped off at a new station in Holland. It's time to change trains. Though our family has two decades of experience with ASD, it's hard to envision the future and plan for it.

I believe that Greg will live a long, happy life. He has good skills. But he'll need support for the rest of his life. Adulthood and ASD is a whole new realm for us. Then there's that pesky mortality thing – we must face the fact that Greg's Mom and Dad won't always be here. That's the scariest part of this new journey. It's one thing to conquer potty training, simple math or a social skill. Quite another to set up a support structure for your adult child that must endure after you're gone.

Ready or not, the train is rolling. It's leaving the station. There's nothing to do but hop on and try to enjoy the ride.

Chapter 2: Greg's World

Autism is a spectrum disorder. People with autism are a diverse group with common traits. Thinking of a spectrum or continuum is a useful way to view this population. Make no mistake: every person with ASD is unique. What works for one might not work for the next. And another thing: every person with ASD is talented.

The first descriptions of what is now called ASD were published nearly 70 years ago. In 1943, an Austrian doctor named Leo Kanner described autism while working as the Director of Child Psychiatry at Johns Hopkins Hospital in Baltimore. In German, "aut" means inward. Dr. Kanner used the word autism to describe children who were inwardly absorbed and didn't relate well to the outside world.

One year later in Vienna, another Austrian doctor, Hans Asperger, described a syndrome for a group of young patients who didn't socialize and had intense absorption in a special interest. He called these children "little professors." People with Asperger's Syndrome are now included on the autism spectrum.

Greg is in the middle of the spectrum. He has functional language, but can't fully converse with you. His vocabulary is sufficient for him to communicate his wants and needs. He answers simple questions with a yes or no. Conversations with him are brief, often repetitive.

He gives me on the spot, turn-by-turn navigation to a store or restaurant ten miles from our house, but can't safely get across the street or through a crowded parking lot. He cares deeply for his mother, sister and father, but doesn't express that affection in normal ways.

Like most people with ASD, Greg has unusual attachments to certain topics and objects. The obsessions have changed over the years. They've strengthened, then weakened. New obsessions have come to the surface. Lining up or stacking objects. Collecting certain kinds of books or movies. Recently, we finally extinguished Greg's habit of taking a paper napkin from every place he went – restaurant, house, gas station, school. He'd collect the napkins all day, put them under his pillow while he slept at night, and throw them away the next morning. Once a month, we'd find ourselves in a mini-crisis because one of the napkins went missing.

The simplest description of autism is that it's a wiring problem. Physiological. Neurobiological. The brains of people with ASD are wired differently. They process sensory input differently. They have "splinter skills" – things they do extremely well. These strengths are counterbalanced by significant deficits in other areas.

The symbol of autism is the puzzle piece. It's a mysterious condition. How in the world can Raymond Babbitt, a.k.a. "Rain Man," instantaneously count the toothpicks that just fell on the floor? How can my son remember details of things we did 15 years ago? The mystery is deepened because, despite accelerated research, there is still no known cause or cure for autism.

We do a great disservice to people with ASD if we focus only on their remarkable displays of memory or other peculiar talents. I recently saw a TV news story about a workplace for people with disabilities. Very positive story. Until the end, when it focused on a special skill of a young man with ASD. Give him a date, and he'll tell you what day of the week it was. The TV reporter mentioned his own birth date in 1951. The young man told him that the date was a Sunday. That became the highlight of the news story, taking the emphasis away from the overall achievements of that group of workers.

If we see people with ASD only as carnival acts, we miss their larger accomplishments. Not the least of which is this: The world they live in isn't created for them. It's for us "normal" people. People who aren't bothered by the high-pitched whine of a vacuum cleaner. People who understand that when the power goes out, the television doesn't work, so we can't watch *Jeopardy!*. People who aren't deeply troubled if their shirt sleeve gets a little damp from a spill.

If we let people with ASD design a world for themselves, it would be a much different place. Orderly. Predictable.

Comforting. But they weren't given that chance to design an ASD-friendly world. We shoehorn them into our world. That they survive at all is an accomplishment beyond any I'll ever achieve.

Come to think of it, Autism Spectrum Disorder is quite a misnomer. A person with autism values order above most anything else.

I've read a few news articles and books reporting a case in which a child's autism has been "cured." Often, a specific therapy is attributed to the cure. I'm genuinely happy for a good outcome for any child with ASD. On the other hand, my experience makes me a skeptic. Even if those stories are accurate, the "cure" doesn't represent a silver bullet, a simple path that will work for all people across the autism spectrum.

As parents, we become obsessed. Obsessed with "fixing" our kids, making them more normal. Educators and medical professionals also have the "fix-it" mentality, to a lesser extent than us parents.

A young woman with ASD was asked the question, "What is normal?" Her reply: "It's a button on the clothes dryer." I reject the idea that we must fix these kids. What right have I to assume that there's a "normal" boy locked inside of my son's ASD? That it's my job to find him? Coincidentally, selfishness on my part would probably lead me to assume that the trapped boy is a lot like me. In other words, if I could just find the "normal" Greg, I'd find someone who reminds me of me.

I suspect that if Greg were able to converse on this topic, he'd tell me to stand down. He'd tell me that he is who he is. We'd make a deal – I wouldn't search for my "normal" son, and he'd accept his father "as is." People with ASD don't need to be made normal. They just need support to help them adapt to our world.

I take issue with another characterization – the idea that we're fighting autism. We may be fighting to find the cause and cure. However, I often see something much different – headlines like "Mother Battles Her Son's Autism." It's common to hear that someone fought a battle with cancer or another disease. I'm uncomfortable with the same notion being applied to autism. Autism is not a disease. Autism is organic. It's part of who Greg is. We haven't fought Greg's autism all these years. We've adapted to it. In turn, we've tried to help him adapt to our world.

Think of it this way: Greg is an ambassador from the world of autism. The rest of us in his family are ambassadors from the "normal" world. We've spent our lives learning each other's ways, appreciating each other's culture and treasuring the humanity that underlies all of our differences.

Part 2

Growing Up

From birth to diagnosis to high school graduation, countless lessons for him and for us.

Chapter 3: Early Years

Greg was our first child. As rookie parents, Doreen and I had no real idea of developmental milestones. Even if we'd had more experience, nothing in his first year would have tipped us off about his ASD.

He was a beautiful baby. Our next-door neighbor at his birth, now a friend forever, told us that seeing baby Greg helped her decide to have children herself.

We have lots of home video of him. At two months, he smiled and made eye contact. His physical development was on track. He began walking right on time. He could tell us the sounds that a sheep and a cow make. There was one unusual trait: he sometimes arched his back to draw away from the person holding him. Due to this, his aunt gave him the nickname "Archie." Other than that, he was appropriately affectionate and seemed happy.

Changes began in his second year. I'd come home from work and find him watching a video or playing in the family room. I'd call his name, but he wouldn't respond.

Home video shows him playing with toys in unusual ways. Constantly stacking, lining up and counting things. His speech regressed. He said fewer words. Eye contact disappeared. We made regular visits to the pediatrician. When we'd ask about the symptoms we were seeing, the doctor said that all children develop differently.

Here, our story matches the stories of thousands of other parents of children with ASD. With all of the advances in autism research in the last 20 years, there are still well intentioned doctors giving that same advice, which amounts to, "Don't worry about it." Don't accept that answer. Challenge your doctor. If you're not satisfied, find another doctor. Better yet, find a clinic that can evaluate specifically for ASD.

We found an experienced psychologist at The Ohio State University who diagnosed Greg through observation. On April 9, 1990, when Greg was 2 years old, we received the bad news.

Now, I'm not a guy who cries easily. I can only remember crying over Greg three times. The first time was when we received that diagnosis. Doreen and I got back into our car in the parking garage and had a good cry. We felt as though our dreams for our son's future were shattered. As Ms. Kingsley wrote in her essay, "The loss of that dream is a very significant loss."

Greg's first diagnosis was PDD-NOS, meaning, "pervasive developmental disorder not otherwise specified." Sounded like mumbo-jumbo to us, and it still does. We met with other medical specialists. In January 1992, a doctor in Cleveland, Ohio, became the first professional to write the word "autism" in a report about Greg.

Since there's no surefire way to diagnose autism, some doctors might hesitate to apply that label to a child. For us, the label was useful. It gave us a field to explore. We also felt it was important in the school setting. We could use the latest information about autism to help develop Greg's educational services. We could do our part to make the special education demographic statistics more precise, for the benefit of all children with ASD.

As we were beginning to have concerns about Greg's development, our family grew by one. Anne was born when Greg was 22 months old. She came to be described as our "typically developing child." From the start, she was destined to be the "big" little sister. The greatest gift that Greg ever received.

Not that he paid her much attention in those early days. She was just another something in the house. Since she didn't move around much for a few months, he could carry on his activities without crossing her path.

Greg's development from toddler to elementary school was eventful. There are numerous incidents that we'll never forget.

He was "squirmy" during diaper changing. In 1989, that tendency landed us on the local police blotter. One evening after dinner, we were playing with him in the family room. We had used the couch cushions to make a fort. Toys were everywhere. As bedtime approached, I took him upstairs to our bedroom to change his diaper and get his pajamas on. To keep him occupied, I handed him the phone from our bedside stand. The kind of phone with dialing buttons on the handset.

What are the odds that Greg's small fingers would happen to touch the "9" key once and the "1" key twice? The 911 emergency operator heard only the screaming and fussing of a young boy who wasn't enjoying his diaper change – and sprang into action.

Local law enforcement responded swiftly. As we later learned from our neighbors, several cruisers sped toward our house in stealth mode, without sirens or flashing lights. The officers walked around the outside of the house. Through a back window, they could see a family room in disarray with pillows, cushions and toys strewn about.

Weapons drawn, they knocked on the front door. Doreen was several months pregnant with Anne at the time. When she opened the door, she got the shock of her life. It took several minutes for us to prove to them that the child in the house was not in danger. As we talked to the officers, Greg wandered out to the top of the steps, in plain view from the doorway below. The lead officer asked, "Ma'am, is that the child?" Oh yeah, that's him.

We bought *Sesame Street* videos and Greg watched them over and over, memorizing the songs and skits. Jumping, shouting and falling down on cue with the characters he was watching. He loved the show's focus on numbers and letters. We bought him an ABC puzzle: wooden letters about two inches tall that fit into a wooden base. One afternoon, I sat in the family room watching television while Greg played on the floor. He removed the A from the puzzle base and set it on the floor. Next, he removed the B and placed it below and to the right of the A. He continued alphabetically, and the final result was 26 mixed-up letters in three horizontal lines.

As he was finishing, I noticed that the sequence of the letters looked familiar. Then it clicked – he had replicated a computer keyboard. There was no keyboard in the room for him to model or copy. He had the layout in his head! I couldn't do that today if you gave me 50 chances.

While I was a contributor to the family room mess in the 911 incident, Greg could do well creating chaos all by himself, especially in his own bedroom at naptime and at night. It took a long time for him to settle into sleep, and he'd occupy the time by emptying his dresser drawers, removing the drawers from the unit, taking his sheets off the mattress and pulling the mattress off the bed. We took some pictures of this carnage. Now we look back at those photos with amazement.

As a young child, Greg was a "stripper" at bedtime. He didn't like the sensation of a wet diaper, so he'd take off his pajamas and diaper. Doreen tried to outsmart him. When she put him to bed, she'd sew a few stitches just below the neckline to prevent him from unzipping his one-piece pajama suit. That worked for a time. Then he performed an amazing feat that would have made Harry Houdini proud. Though he was zipped and sewn in, he wriggled his arm out of the pajama sleeve, took off his diaper, and removed it though the sleeve.

Potty training isn't easy for children with ASD. Greg wasn't fully trained until age four, and only then because of Doreen's efforts. We kept trying and failing until Doreen decided that this was going to be the day. She had plenty of incentive. As I just mentioned, Greg would strip off his pajamas and diapers. He'd also use the semi-solid material in his used diaper to finger paint his bedroom walls. Most often, the awful clean up duty for that fell to Doreen. So one day she put him on the toilet seat and stayed there with him for almost an hour. She said Greg was quite afraid, to the point that his knees were shaking. He overcame those fears and her efforts were rewarded. We ended up getting both kids out of diapers at the same time.

Greg eventually stopped trashing his bedroom. That was the good news. The bad news was that, around the age of six, he became adept at escaping from it. We tried to stay one step ahead in this battle of wits, resorting to switching the doorknob so it locked from the outside.

We forgot about the windows.

One morning we woke up and things seemed normal. His bedroom door was closed and locked, so we assumed he was in there. We found him at the kitchen table, calmly eating dry cereal. Mulch, leaves and small twigs clung to his pajamas. The front door was ajar. He had matching bruises halfway up the back of his calves. The only explanation was that he had unlocked and opened one of his bedroom windows, jumped down a full story into the garden below, and came back into the house through an unlocked front door. We thanked our lucky stars that the incident didn't get reported to child protective services. We did take him to the doctor, and were relieved that he had no real injuries. From then on, we bolted his bedroom windows shut. To this day, we're not sure what happened that morning.

Besides securing his bedroom doors and windows, we had to devise other security measures during his younger days. We raised the chain lock on our front door, out of his reach. As we finished this simple project, we watched Greg pull a stool over to the door, hop up on it, and unfasten the chain. We had more success with our method to secure the refrigerator door. We bought a wide strap, like the kind you'd see on a moving company's dolly. Greg couldn't undo the knotted strap.

For a short time, Greg took to self-injury. Sitting in his locked bedroom, he would bang the back of his head against the wall. The drywall condition progressed from dimples to dents to gaping holes. This was the second time I cried about Greg. I begged him, “Hit me instead of yourself.”

Our pediatrician gave us good advice, although it was hard to follow. He compared Greg’s head banging to crying and advised us to reassure him, but let him be. Fortunately, this behavior disappeared quickly.

I hit Greg once. Literally, a slap on the wrist. One of his favorite *Sesame Street* characters was Guy Smiley, who called himself “America’s Favorite Game Show Host.” At the beginning of each skit, Guy would emerge from behind stage curtains. The curtains fascinated Greg. It must have been an exciting visual stimulus. So he copied it. He got all wound up in the living room drapes, then emerged, saying, “Game Show Host!” Our drapes were getting wrinkled, and I was worried that he’d pull them completely off the wall. In a stern voice, I told him “No.” He did it again. I gave him a light slap on the wrist. He looked at me oddly. Then he went back into the curtains, reemerged and held out his hand for me to slap again. I swallowed hard.

Outings with Greg were risky because he was prone to tantrums. One day, Doreen took both kids to the grocery store. It was a bad day. Greg was screaming and acting up in Aisle 6, while baby Anne was sitting in the shopping cart. Most parents in this situation would be frustrated, angry and embarrassed. But as always, Doreen handled it well.

One fellow shopper, an anonymous angel, stopped to help.

She said to Doreen, "Hang in there, Mom. You're doing a good job." Her words touched Doreen deeply. To this day, Doreen turns the tables and tries to be the comforter whenever she sees a parent struggling with an unhappy child. My wife can't pay that kind woman back. Instead, she pays it forward.

Chapter 4: School Days

Greg entered preschool special education at age three. At first, he was in a county program located in a school about ten miles from our house. Once he reached elementary-school age, he was placed in our neighborhood public school. We felt lucky to live in Central Ohio. Even way back in the olden days – the early 1990s – the Dublin City School District provided great services for children with special needs.

My own early school years were in the mid-1960s. Like most other baby boomers, I had no exposure to special education students. They were relegated to separate facilities. They rode there on special buses. They weren't included in the community. I think of the pioneers of the early 1970s, like Ruth Sullivan, who pushed for better ways to educate children with disabilities. Their efforts have directly benefited thousands of kids like Greg and their families.

Thanks to them, there's a federal special education law known as the Individuals with Disabilities Education Act

(IDEA). Under this law, each student with a disability is entitled to a free and appropriate public education in the least restrictive environment possible. A team that includes the parents and the student makes decisions about placement, curriculum and services. Each year, together with teachers, therapists and school administrators, the family creates an Individualized Education Program (IEP) for their child. The goal is consensus among the team of educators and family. There are many factors to consider and opportunities for conflict.

Most parents and education professionals believe that kids with disabilities should be fully included in regular classrooms, mixed in with the "regular" kids. The theory is that the special needs kids benefit from having typical peer models, and the normal kids grow in awareness and acceptance of differences.

Doreen and I believe in inclusion. We're also realistic. We couldn't see Greg comprehending subjects like history. We thought he'd do better in a smaller setting with five to eight classmates, as opposed to 25–30. His expressive language developed slowly, so he needed speech therapy. He also needed occupational therapy. We felt Greg would be best served in a classroom with a trained special education teacher, classroom aides (now called paraprofessionals) and therapists. We kept him in this type of setting through his entire academic career, which consisted of 22 placements over 19 years. He was included in some regular classes – like art, gym, music, computers and shop – an hour or two each day.

When Greg was diagnosed, we got involved in a local support group, a chapter of the Autism Society of America. It was helpful to compare notes with other parents, especially those whose children were a little older. We got lots of good advice about the IEP process. We learned that a school district with limited resources, or worse, with limited understanding of the issues, could try to railroad families into certain placements or services. And that parents who approached their districts with unrealistic demands could jeopardize the consensus process.

If the IEP team reaches an impasse, there's an administrative appeals process. After that, the matter can be taken to court. One experienced support group member told us that, even though Greg probably wouldn't go to college, we should still set aside the funds we would have used for college tuition. That money could pay for legal services in a battle with our school district. Another old-timer had some simpler advice. She found it was much easier to use honey than vinegar. In other words, as parents we should be well prepared but amicable. Don't walk in the door with guns blazing.

We used the honey approach. Not to say that we agreed with every one of the school district's suggestions. We stood our ground when needed. We felt strongly that Greg needed speech and occupational therapy. We made sure that the IEP specifically listed the frequency of those services. In the end, we were always able to achieve consensus with our cooperative school district.

Greg had one bad school placement. Since we were part of the decision-making process, the mistake was as much ours as the school district's. When he was eight years old, the age when he was perhaps the most defiant, we put him in what was then called an SBH class. This stood for "severe behavior handicap." The idea was for students to "earn" their way into regular classes. I don't believe Greg understood the reward concept. He didn't make much progress that year. We had no trouble working with the school district to get him back into a more appropriate placement the next year.

One poor placement out of 22 works out to a 96% success rate. Not bad. Of course, in the moment, a school year that's not going well seems like a catastrophe to the parents. With time comes perspective.

Greg received exceptional service from the teachers, aides, therapists and administrators who came into his life. He gave them many challenges during his early school years. When he was frustrated, he would bite. He'd also make like a wrestler and employ a head butt.

Greg was also a "runner." Left unattended, he'd scamper down the hallway or try to escape across the playground during recess. The school gym was a popular destination; the curtains on the stage made for great Guy Smiley skits. Every class picture during this period shows Greg positioned right next to or in front of a teacher or aide applying a firm grip to keep him in place.

Recently, Greg and I were looking at those old class pictures. One showed a small class, just seven kids, a teacher and an aide. Greg looked at the picture and a smirk grew on his face. Pointing his finger, one by one, to people in the photo, he said, "Hit, hit, push, hit, push." He remembers his aggressive days in elementary school. More amazingly, he remembers which fellow students or school staff he hit, and which ones he pushed. He knows now that the behavior isn't acceptable. Yet he retains vivid memories and finds humor in them.

Autism is a developmental disability. People with ASD have developmental delays – cognitive or other skills that take longer to develop. In some areas, it's not just a delay; it's more like a developmental absence. Yet, some skill development isn't delayed at all; it's accelerated. With Greg, the best example was his fine motor skill.

This skill developed quickly in his preschool years, as teachers presented him with paper and a writing instrument. He had no trouble finding a comfortable and effective grip. He became a combination artist and visual journalist, and he took up a new hobby honing those skills at home.

He wanted markers and paper. Lots of them. We had buckets full of markers and reams of paper. He'd sit at a table or on the floor for hours, drawing pictures and writing words. We saved some of his work product – in storage bins in our basement. A couple of his creations rose to a more lofty status. They're framed and on display.

The first is Greg's rendition of the stage at our local Chuck E. Cheese restaurant, circa 1995, drawn with colored markers on an 18 x 24 inch piece of paper. He created the picture at home, freehand, with no picture to copy from. The drawing shows five puppet characters. The likeness is good enough, although the artistry is definitely childish. Interestingly to me, all five characters seem to be looking in the same direction, slightly to the right. But the real story of the picture is the additional detail.

He reproduced everything else on that stage: the characters' microphones and instruments, the city scene buildings in the backdrop, the sign reading "Munch's Make Believe Band," a speaker hanging from the ceiling, an analog clock with the hands showing 10:30, even an electrical plug on the floor.

The next time we went to Chuck E. Cheese, I took a close look at the stage. I was amazed to find that all the elements on the set matched Greg's drawing exactly, in both relative size and placement. This is a classic example of his extraordinary memory, his remarkable visual sense.

The second piece of Greg's framed art is a sequence of six drawings, each on a separate sheet of 8 1/2 x 11 paper. The first sheet shows two popsicles in plain wrappers. The next shows the wrappers flying off, exposing two yellow popsicles. The next three sheets show the treats slowly disappearing, with more of the popsicle sticks showing on each successive drawing. The final sheet shows just the two sticks. When he finished, I asked him, "Greg, what is this?" He replied, "Yellow ice cream is all gone." I thought that was pretty cool. We put all six drawings in a frame, had Greg write his title on it, and gave it to his Grandpa and Grandma.

In addition to drawing, Greg developed extremely fine penmanship. He's always been quite a perfectionist, whether printing or writing in cursive. My own handwriting never was very good, and it gets worse every year. Greg is the opposite. His writing is nearly the quality of calligraphy.

His gross motor skills weren't advanced, but they developed normally. He's never done much in sports, because the rules are too abstract for him to understand. He is a decent swimmer. In his preschool years, we found a program that subsidized swim lessons for kids with disabilities. He received one-on-one instruction from a great swim teacher whom he called "Miss Ann." We were proud to see his progress from a full vest to arm "swimmies" to swimming on his own. This opened the door to a lifetime of enjoyment for Greg. These days, he likes to go to the community pool, where he'll jump off the diving board four times – never more, never less. He especially enjoys going to the beach, where the tactile and visual stimulation of the incoming waves mesmerize him. When we drive past the building where he took swim lessons 20 years ago, he still remarks, "Greg swim class. Miss Ann."

Occupational therapy was important to Greg during this time. People with ASD usually have acute sensory needs. For Greg, two things were especially helpful in keeping him calm. He enjoyed being rolled up in a mat like a hot dog or being buried under a beanbag. The "closed-in" feeling was comforting for him. His teachers and therapists used the mats and beanbag for "sensory breaks" when Greg was agitated or frustrated. This technique parallels a key element of the story in Claire Danes' Emmy-winning portrayal of Temple Grandin, a highly successful and celebrated adult with ASD. Ms. Grandin invented a "squeeze machine" to help herself cope with stress. She's a true legend in the ASD world, and it's great that Hollywood told her story in the recent HBO movie.

Greg had a similar routine at home. He went through a phase of wanting to climb into bed and pull the covers completely over himself. He'd do this alone or with whoever else was in the room. More than once, he surprised a first-time visitor to our house by coaxing the visitor to his bedroom and directing them into his bed. He still sleeps this way, under the covers from head to toe. But he no longer looks for others to participate.

Greg's second comforting sensory aid was smooth fabrics. He'd carry around fragments of silk clothing and ribbons. Rubbing them between his fingers helped him to stay calm and centered. In a department store, he'd make a beeline for the lingerie section. He still does this. Try explaining why your 23-year-old son is fondling silky women's undergarments under your supervision!

Those early years were challenging, but Greg made good progress. With the help of the school staff, he grew his cognitive skills, improved his behavior and started to acquire better social skills. His personality emerged more clearly. Greg was a busy little boy. He was also teachable, loyal, funny and resourceful.

One example of Greg's resourcefulness happened during a standardized test. When he was about nine years old, the school psychologist administered a few tests for use in his educational assessment. In the vocabulary section, one question showed a drawing of an overweight person. Three words were printed below the drawing, and Greg was to circle the correct word. His choices were: cat, fat and hat.

This stumped him. Neither his teachers nor we had ever taught him the concept of someone being fat. He quickly fashioned a solution. He drew a hat on top of the head of the person in the drawing. Then he circled the word "hat." The psychologist who told us this story praised his thinking. At the same time, she said that according to the rules of the standardized test, she had to mark his answer incorrect. This is a classic example of how a person with ASD is required to conform to our world. His answer was correct. He lives in a world that says his answer was wrong.

Greg's test story reminds me of another example of entirely logical behavior by a person with ASD. A friend of mine has a grandson on the spectrum. She told me about his first experience playing "buddy baseball" – basically little league adapted for kids with disabilities, with typical peer buddies on the field to help out. As her grandson Sam was about to play his first game, his father took a minute to review the key points. He said to his son, "Now, remember to touch every base." Sam made good contact in his first at bat, and began to circle the bases. Thing was, he stopped at each base to reach down and touch it – with his hand!

Chapter 5: Calendars and Change

Autism is often associated with routine and resistance to change. In his last three years of elementary school and four years of middle school, Greg had to change buildings and teachers just once. His calendar skills improved. He became accustomed to a sequence and pace of life. School starting in August. Trick or Treat in October. Thanksgiving and winter breaks. New Year's Day. The St. Patrick's Day parade. (Remember, we live in Dublin, Ohio, and Doreen's maiden name is Connelly. March 17 is a big date in our house.) Easter in the spring. School ending in early June. Summer camps. Fireworks on the 4th of July. School restarting in August.

Our family calendar has always been on our kitchen counter. Greg keeps an eye on it. He can read and understand the entries for out-of-town trips to visit relatives and friends. He's the one who reminds us that I have a dentist appointment or Doreen has book club tomorrow.

We found that sticking to a routine made for a more peaceful family existence. We used this approach not just for seasonal events, but also for daily activity. Living with a person with ASD makes you a planning expert. Thinking a few steps ahead to try to ensure that things will unfold predictably. The primary objective is to avoid the meltdown or tantrum that might occur with an unexpected change or disappointment.

We lived that structure and routine through Greg's adolescence. Then we diverted – in a big way. My job required us to move from Central Ohio to Birmingham, Alabama. Leaving the home base that Greg had known for all of his 16 years. Moving 600 miles and four states away. This meant a new house, new school district, new camps, and so on. The first large-scale transition of Greg's life. We had to think long and hard on how to introduce this change to him.

Like most people with ASD, Greg is literal and visual. Explaining that we were moving to another state wouldn't mean much to him. We could show him Alabama on a map, but we weren't confident of his map skills. We needed to make the explanation concrete, not abstract. We decided to get things set up and then break the news to him.

Our move occurred during the summer. Doreen insisted that our family be in Birmingham before the first day of school. That gave us six weeks, from early July to mid-August, to make the arrangements. We scouted the area, selected a school district and then began to house hunt. We found a house, but couldn't take possession until late September. We also arranged for some temporary housing.

We took Greg with us on the last scouting trip. We drove around the town with him. Took him inside his new school and met his new teacher, although we didn't explain that to him at that time. After a day of exploring the new area, we returned to our hotel where Doreen and I told him about the upcoming change.

We'd brought along our January-December family calendar, a new August-July school-year calendar, and photographs of the new house, the temporary house and the new school. Sitting on the floor of the hotel room with Greg's silky comfort items close by, we let him know about the big change. We started by tearing out the last five months of our family calendar. Then we wrote entries into the new calendar. The date that we'd move to Alabama. The date that school started there. The date for trick-or-treating in our new neighborhood. We showed Greg pictures of his new environment that matched his experience of driving around that day.

Greg was shaken; his heart was beating fast. For about an hour, he kept talking about his surroundings in Ohio – house, school, etc. He wanted to look at the events on the torn-out calendar pages. We kept our voices calm and low. We focused on the new calendar. We pointed to pictures of the new school. We put the silky comfort items in his hands.

Soon it was time for bed. We went through Greg's normal routine, and he settled into the hotel bed. Doreen and I looked at each other and wondered what the next morning would hold.

Our fears were unfounded. He woke up the next morning fully accepting the new plan. He did refer to the old school and house - in a joking way. Looking back, I realize this is when Greg began to use humor as a means of coping with change. Today, he'll repeat information that he knows to be wrong and laugh when we correct him.

We lived in Birmingham for three years, then moved back to Central Ohio. In retrospect, this change was not that big a deal for Greg. Because of his socialization deficits, he acknowledges no real friends. Therefore, as long as we can explain changes in structure and routine in a way he understands, he's okay. The second time around, for the return move to Ohio, Greg knew what the packing, the boxes, and the moving truck meant. He stood in front of the Alabama house and said, "Bye-bye Lake Run Drive. We will miss you!"

The biggest lesson Greg learned from our moves was simply that things could change. Now, when his favorite TV show is preempted, he'll say, "They changed it," and get a good laugh from the unexpected occurrence.

The experience of moving taught the rest of us much more. A household with ASD can become imprisoned by structure. We learned that Greg was more adaptable than we had given him credit for.

Chapter 6: First Work Experiences

In his last years in middle school, Greg's IEP goals shifted from academics to functional life skills and vocational training. We were lucky that our school districts in Ohio and Alabama were open to this.

Greg's vocational training started when he learned to shelve books in the middle school library. Melvil Dewey may have created an arcane library filing system, but in the end, it's just alphabetized letters and sequenced numbers. Hundreds of hours of *Sesame Street* viewing had prepared Greg well. Lining up books on shelves played to his strengths. He understood and took to the work. The staff at the school told us that they could always tell where Greg had been working: The books were lined up perfectly straight, flush with the front edge of the shelf.

Greg started work-study in community settings during his first year of high school. It was an hour or two per day, a couple of days per week. He was supported by a job coach or a teacher's aide provided by the school district. His first outside work assignment was at a JC Penney store at the local mall. What did he do there? That's what I wanted to know after his first day on the job.

Me: "Did you go to JC Penney today?"

Greg: "Yes."

Me: "What did you do there?"

Greg: "To work."

Me: "Yes, Greg is working at JC Penney. What did you *do* at JC Penney?"

Greg: "It's all inside."

Me: [suppressing laughter] "Yes, that's what the JC Penney signs say. Greg is working. What did you do?"

Greg: "Small, medium, large, XL."

This interaction speaks volumes about ASD. Greg's visual sense is amazingly acute. Of course, there were signs throughout the JC Penney store that bore their slogan: "It's All Inside." To Greg, that phrase was the key feature of the place. Getting any more information from him was like pulling teeth. He finally let me know about the clothes sizes, so I assumed he was organizing apparel.

Greg doesn't think the way I do. He lives in the moment. He thinks about the future, but only in terms of events that will occur. As for the past, it's passed. He knew I hadn't been there while he was working, and he probably had no idea why I'd be interested in knowing what went on.

As Greg's high school years progressed, he had many

other opportunities to demonstrate and strengthen his work skills. Data entry in a mall office. Office filing at a temporary agency. Data entry for a large non-profit organization. Stocking items at a bookstore. Shelving books at a community library. Printing and binding in the school district's central office. Rolling silverware in napkins at a restaurant. Custodial cleaning at a health club.

I tried to drag out of Greg what one of his data entry jobs entailed. All I got was, "Type numbers." Imagine my surprise when I found out that the job required him to find a code on a book cover, consult a thick binder, cross-reference the book's code to some other information in the binder, and then enter or delete information in a database. The key to Greg's success on this job was that the vocational support staff was able to take a complex job and break it down into a series of steps. Greg learned each step well. As a result, he mastered the entire process.

For six school years, Greg built his resume. Proving he has the skills to add value in a variety of work settings. Repetition and accuracy are his strengths. Communication and socialization — especially understanding social context — are big challenges. Greg's a back-office type, not a front-counter guy.

All the employers in Greg's work-study programs were great. His work assignments were preplanned and short-term. Good training, but the environments were still somewhat artificial. The real test came later when he transitioned to a paying job.

Chapter 7: Family

Raising a child with ASD puts unusual stress on a family. There's a myth that the divorce rate in ASD families is higher than in the general population. I read an article that provided statistics to dispel that myth. The divorce rate is nearly the same as for the general population.

We've circulated in the ASD community for more than 20 years. We've met many single mothers raising a child with ASD. Never met a single father, only single mothers. It must be unbelievably difficult to take on the challenge alone.

For the most part, I subscribe to the adage, "Judge not, lest you be judged." I'm sure there are lots of reasons why marriages fail. Perhaps having a child with ASD magnifies trouble that already exists in a relationship. However, on a few occasions, I've heard an explanation that makes my blood boil. It comes from the father who walks away from his child with ASD, saying, "This isn't what I signed up for."

Are you kidding me? This isn't a church bazaar where you sign up for a booth, or a neighborhood block watch where you take your shift. Buddy, you chose to have or adopt a child. You signed up for that, and nobody made you any promises about how it would work out. Even if the marriage doesn't last, how about you man up and lend a real helping hand? [End of rant.]

Growing up as a sibling of a child with ASD is a challenge. When it comes to siblings, Greg hit the jackpot. His younger sister is many things to him: teacher, protector, comforter and co-conspirator. In two decades in the ASD community, we've found that ASD sibs are remarkable people. And they have special needs of their own.

It's been fascinating to watch Anne's relationship with Greg. She was an active child, right from the start. As soon as she started to walk and talk, she took control. She was spunky. She didn't need to adjust to Greg. She took him as she found him. At age three, her social and intellectual skills had surpassed her older brother. She started running interference for him. We remember a grocery shopping trip around that time. As we were checking out, Greg displayed odd behavior. Anne told the cashier, "He has autism."

We called our daughter "Annie" until age seven, when she told us she'd prefer to go by her given name, Anne. Greg got an exemption from this change. He was allowed to continue to call her Annie. Still does.

The advice for parents of special needs children is to make

time for the other children in the family – the ones without special needs. Good advice, and we followed it by carving out "solo time" with Anne. Taking short out-of-town trips, just the three of us. Once in a while, attending her extra-curricular activities without Greg.

Nonetheless, the vast majority of our time was spent together as a family. And our family reality is what Anne came to know. She participated on a sibling panel at an autism conference when she was ten years old. I'll tell you that she did better than the other, much older panel members.

Early on, we decided to send Greg and Anne to different schools. They are separated by just 22 months and one school year. We didn't want Anne to feel the need to watch over Greg at school. She needed to find her own way, make her own friends.

Anne's early adolescent years were the hardest. I think they are for all children. Social acceptance is critical to a "tweenager." It's natural that Anne's relationship with Greg was strained in this period. His behavior was more likely to embarrass her when we were out in public. Yet even during this time, when she was at home with Greg, she gave him great support and encouragement.

She needed some space, and we gave it to her. Soon, she started to ask more mature questions about her brother. We began to let her watch Greg for a short time while we ran an errand. By the time we moved to Alabama – on Anne's 15th birthday – she had come back around to unconditional acceptance of her brother. She had also set her mind on what career path she'd take: a special education teacher or some other profession to serve people with disabilities.

In Alabama, Greg and Anne did go to the same school. By then, Anne had matured to the point of being a third parent. In one of her first days at the Alabama high school, she heard a PA announcement that a boy from a certain class was "on the loose." Anne guessed that the boy might be Greg, and asked permission to join the search. As it turned out, he had gone to the restroom. He calmly walked out and headed back to his classroom. Anne shrugged her shoulders and returned to hers.

Now, that ponytailed girl has grown up to be an impressive young woman. With a special education degree from The Ohio State University, she's already making a difference in the lives of other families affected by ASD. Anne participated in another ASD sibling panel not long ago. One of the women in the audience asked her a simple, but desperately important question: "Will my other child [the one without autism] love me?" In other words: "I know that I'm giving a lot of time and effort to my child with ASD. Will his brother or sister resent me for that?" Anne assured the mother that things would be just fine.

Beginning college, she looked at Greg as a brother first, but also as a case study. She gave us helpful suggestions. At Anne's urging, we found ways to extinguish some of Greg's obsessive behaviors that were dominating portions of our lives. A bit unnerving to have your daughter critiquing your parenting skills. But I have to say, she's often right. We're not the only ones who get to hear her opinion. If you visit Anne's Facebook page, you'll be politely asked to avoid using the "R" word, and to visit www.r-word.org.

The topic of siblings brings to mind an issue that I've struggled with. I'll feel better for making this confession. Like anyone else, I'm always meeting new people — at work, in the neighborhood, etc. Even if it's just a passing acquaintance, it's natural for the initial discussion to turn to family. When I'm asked if I have children, I'll sometimes take a minimalist approach — I respond that we have a son and a daughter, mention their ages, and offer no more details. It's not that I'm at all ashamed of my son. Rather, I sometimes just want to avoid having to explain about Greg's autism.

This approach rarely works. My new acquaintance will invariably ask some follow-up questions, and I'll provide my canned response that describes Greg: "No, he's not in college or married. He has a disability called autism. He's doing very well."

Greg's extended family has been a blessing to all of us. Grandparents, aunts, uncles, cousins and many others. They've also been involved in Greg's more humorous events and teachable moments.

When Greg was five, we took a trip to a local theme park with Doreen's family. Including our kids, there were seven cousins no more than six years apart. Three of Doreen's sisters, their spouses, and Grandpa and Grandma were also there. We arranged to meet at the water fountain near the park entrance. As we began to gather, Matthew, one of Greg's cousins, stood on the concrete ledge that surrounded the fountain. Greg walked up and pushed him into the fountain! Matt was now wet and unhappy. Luckily, we had brought a change of clothes for Greg that also fit Matt. The group picture we took on that fateful day shows Matt decked out in Greg's spare duds.

To this day, Greg still fondly remembers that incident. He'll get a devious grin on his face and say to me, "Matthew is pushing." (Translation: "I pushed Matthew.") I'll say, "No pushing Matthew," and he chuckles. Greg repeats the same words in Matthew's presence. This is even funnier these days, because Greg is 5'7" and 120 pounds and Matt is about 6'2" and 185. Today, Greg couldn't push Matt over. Matt's a good sport about his cousin's long memory of the incident.

Our family gave Greg his first lessons about death. In 2000, he lost his maternal grandfather and a paternal great-grandmother in the space of two months. Both were hospitalized before they passed away. Greg, Anne and all their cousins had the opportunity to visit their Grandpa in the hospital and say a touching goodbye.

Greg attended both wakes and funerals. We did the best we could to explain death to him. The final result of our teaching is a script that he still repeats when we look at a picture of Grandpa or drive through Doreen's parents' old neighborhood: "Grandpa is sick. Hospital. He died. He's gone. Grandpa in heaven."

A short while later, Doreen caught a cold. I wanted to let her recover, so I tried to stay out of her way, and encouraged Greg to do the same. I told him that Mom was sick. He got a strange look on his face. Then I remembered the script sequence: "sick-hospital-died ..." Since then, we've stopped using the term "sick." We also had to help him understand that someone could go into the hospital and come back home without dying.

In 2002, two years after Greg's grandfather and great-grandmother died, a co-worker's mother passed away. I went to the wake to pay my respects. Doreen and Greg came with me. At the time, he was still in his "bed/covers" phase, enjoying the closed-in sensation of being under the covers with another person. At the wake, the casket lid was open during visiting hours.

Greg looked at the scene. His eyes fixed on the silky casket lining. He said, "Greg and lady is sleeping in the box." Meaning, "I'm going to get into the big, soft bed the lady is lying in." Fortunately, I had a grip on his hand. It took all my strength to keep him in place. I explained that it wasn't going to happen, and we shortened our stay in order to remove the temptation.

Greg is just now exploring the concept that someday he

and his sister, Mom and Dad won't be around. He knows the years in which we were all born, so if he sees in print the year 1975, he'll say "One Dad, one Mom, zero Greg, zero Annie." Or he'll reference the year 2900 and then say, "Zero Dad, zero Mom, zero Greg, zero Annie."

The problem is that Greg really wants to know exactly when we'll all go from alive ("one") to not alive ("zero"). He's formed a hypothesis about this, using an unintended source of information.

Following in the steps of a neighbor in her childhood, Doreen began a tradition of having our kids photographed with Santa. Not so unusual, except that she's kept the tradition going for 24 Christmases and intends to keep it going. Greg eagerly anticipates this annual event. Anne doesn't mind playing along. Doreen has made a scrapbook that has each year's Santa picture and the holiday card we mailed out. Each page of the scrapbook, in a laminated plastic sleeve, has that year's picture and card. We bring out the scrapbook each Christmas season and update it with this year's material.

Several times each December, we sit with Greg on the couch and page through the book. He usually recites some fact about each page. For example, the name of the mall where the photo was taken. The scrapbook binder has extra blank laminated sleeves in the back, waiting for the memories of future years.

Here lies the problem. Last year, Greg leafed through

the remaining blank pages, ticking off one year for each laminated sheet. His count, which was 100% accurate, meant that the last sheet would hold memories of the year 2026. Based on that, he reported to us, "2027 – zero Daddy, zero Mommy, zero Greg, zero Annie." Makes perfect sense. No more pages = no more Christmases = no more family.

We've yet to fix that misconception. We either have to add more blank sheets to the scrapbook or find a way to explain that no one knows when their time is up. And further explain that it's not likely that all four of us will disappear in the same year.

Adding more pages will be much easier.

Chapter 8: Community

In two decades of Greg's life, there's been a change for the better in terms of the community's understanding and acceptance of people with ASD. That speaks well of our society as a whole. The change is more dramatic when you look at it over the half century of my lifetime.

When I attended elementary school in the 1960s, our peers with special needs were segregated from the regular population. Special buses, special schools and institutionalization were the norm. In 1968 came a movie called *Charly*, starring Cliff Robertson. Based on a book entitled *Flowers for Algernon*, it told the story of a mentally challenged man, and I can remember it making a big impression on me. It was part of a gradual awakening of awareness in our society.

Things improved at a faster pace in the 1970s, with the highlight being a new federal law promising special needs students equality in education. While change didn't occur overnight, the days of segregating students with disabilities were numbered. By the beginning of the 1980s, students in regular schools were beginning to coexist with their peers who had special needs.

The ASD incidence rate was much lower in the 1980s. But the seeds of autism awareness were taking root. In 1989, Charles Hart wrote the book *Without Reason*. This is an amazing real-life story about how autism affected the author's brother and son. Mr. Hart was born in 1940. His brother was 20 years older, born decades before autism was even described. Mr. Hart relates the struggle of growing up in a family with a much older brother who just wasn't right.

Mr. Hart's son was born in 1970. By that time, while knowledge about autism had advanced, it was still an uncommon disorder. His son also struggled through his early years, and Mr. Hart describes the long, slow process that resulted in an autism diagnosis when his son was eight. Only then did it become obvious that the same diagnosis should be applied to his 58-year-old brother!

The same year that *Without Reason* was published, Bill Christopher, who played Father Mulcahy on the TV series *M*A*S*H*, wrote *Mixed Blessings*, a book about the experiences of his son with ASD. In doing so, he became one of the first of many celebrity parents to speak out.

It took a 1988 movie to spread the word about autism more broadly. Ironically, the real-life "Rain Man," Kim Peek, didn't have Autism Spectrum Disorder. His condition was called FG Syndrome. Yet Dustin Hoffman's portrayal of Raymond Babbitt became the generic depiction of autism. This was good in the sense that autism awareness grew exponentially. It was bad in that the Hollywood version became the stereotype for autism. It left out the important point that people with autism fall across a very broad spectrum.

Now to present day, in the second decade of the 21st century. Those 1980s elementary school students have their own children in school. We're well into the second generation of non-segregated education for special needs students.

This point was brought home to me recently. A co-worker of mine has a typically-developing 13-year-old son. He and his son took a routine trip to the grocery store. As they were loading their bags into the car, the son remarked on the developmentally disabled person who had helped bag their groceries. He told his father that he felt good about shopping at that store because it was providing employment opportunities. The father was proud that his son noticed the situation in the first place.

Greg's experience with schoolmates has been uniformly positive. Especially in the middle and high school years, when the regular students were given an opportunity to "buddy up" with special needs students. They served as tutors in certain classes or simply as friends or partners during an activity, like a school assembly.

For years and years, as we circulated in the community, Greg was recognized by his fellow students. At a grocery store or at the movies, we often heard the hearty greeting: "Hi Greg!" That would be followed by a short conversation, during which Doreen or I would find out who the kid was and how he or she knew our son. Greg didn't give much back to these peers, barely acknowledging their existence and certainly not engaging in any kind of meaningful conversation. As his social skills improved marginally, he might give them a half-hearted handshake upon these chance encounters.

His aloofness seemed to attract his peers. I suppose there was something mysterious about him. They knew him from the school setting. Seeing him in the community was a new perspective. Maybe Greg didn't feel their warmth and acceptance, but Doreen, Anne and I did.

We've lived in five neighborhoods during Greg's life. Always blessed with wonderful neighbors. This was especially important when Greg was in the 5-10 age range. This was a time when he'd wander, exploring on his own without our knowledge or permission. We did our best to keep track of him, but sometimes he escaped while we were distracted.

Once, Greg made his way through a "doggie door" at a house three doors down from us. He appeared in the neighbor's family room, surprising them as they watched television. They greeted him, then called us to come down and retrieve our son.

That same family gave Greg a cherished gift. Knowing Greg's love of *Sesame Street*, Jane made him a life-sized

Guy Smiley. She designed it, stuffed it, sewed it by hand and dressed him like the real Game Show Host. She gave it to Greg at his seventh birthday party, held at the local Chuck E. Cheese. We have priceless home video of that moment. Greg escorted his personal Guy Smiley around the restaurant for a good 15 minutes. The Chuck E. Cheese restaurant interior has a stage and curtains, so Greg could simulate Guy Smiley entering the room. Next, Greg settled into a booth with Guy and read a book. Watching that video again so many years later, it occurs to me that Guy Smiley is Greg's true friend. Greg's face is bright, and he handles Guy in a gentle and very human fashion.

He played with that gift for many years. We still have Guy, tucked away in a basement storage area. The years of wear and tear have left him a bit limp. We really should re-stuff him.

Another neighbor across the street had a door in the back of the house for direct access to the basement. In the basement was the fun room, with a pinball machine, a TV, videocassettes and lots of other stuff that interested Greg. When he went missing one day, we called the neighbor and asked her to check her basement. Sure enough, he'd made himself at home there. He was sitting contentedly on the couch, watching a *Sesame Street* video.

There is a wonderful camp facility in Central Ohio, called Recreation Unlimited, which serves people with special needs. When Greg was 12 years old, Doreen and I overcame our fears and decided to send him to an overnight respite weekend camp. One of our best decisions. A break for both him and us. Greg took to camp like a fish to water. He had no difficulty adapting. He understood that things which were part of the daily routine at home might not be the same at camp – instead, there were new routines.

Greg still attends camp regularly: two-night weekends once per month during the school year and a weeklong session in the summer. He's become a top-notch climber thanks to Recreation Unlimited. They have both an outdoor tower and an indoor climbing wall. Greg's recognized for the speed with which he scampers up those structures.

The counselors at camp are typically college students. They and the regular full-time staff are a second family for Greg. In this setting, we again see his magnetism. Several times, Greg's been assigned to a new counselor who doesn't know him. We drop him off on Friday afternoon, giving the new counselor a three-minute "here's what you need to know about Greg" introduction. When we pick him up Sunday at noon, we're invariably told what a treasure we have. "I love Greg! I hope I have him again next time!"

Getting a babysitter for a child with ASD isn't easy. It's not a job for the 13-year-old down the street. Greg likes to go out, so it's been important for our regular sitters to have wheels. We found a couple of great sources for caregivers. Several have been counselors at camps Greg attended. Another was a teacher's aide in Greg's middle school class.

We also use college students. In Ohio and in Alabama, we posted advertisements for our caregiver position, giving a little background about Greg. We'd always find a few interested and capable college students. Several of them we now consider family friends. One has become a priest. Another has finished her graduate studies in Alabama, and last we heard was in Illinois. We try to keep in touch with them. They enjoy being updated on Greg's progress.

Our family's experience with community was enriched during our time in Alabama. Doreen and I were lifelong Ohioans, Midwesterners through and through. As a family, we spent almost three years in Alabama, long enough for us "Yankees" to get a good taste of Southern culture. As for Greg, the move to Alabama proved he could adapt to big changes. He continued to make good progress during his time in the Heart of Dixie.

The most important thing for Greg was getting him into the new school setting. We enrolled him in Vestavia Hills High School in suburban Birmingham. His second year in a high school placement. At the Dublin, Ohio, schools, he was involved in work-study experiences in the community, concentrating on vocational skills. We found that Vestavia's program wasn't as well developed in this area. Nonetheless, the Vestavia district was very open to expanding the program for Greg and the other students. As a result, Greg continued to build his work skills in a variety of community settings.

One difference we found in Alabama was the presence of church-based programs to support people with disabilities. Some church groups offered Friday evening respite services – providing childcare at the church facilities for several hours. Camp Sumatanga, the weeklong summer camp that Greg attended in Alabama, was also sponsored by a church. Church members volunteered to staff the camp. Greg's counselor was a police officer who took a week of vacation to work at the camp. An unselfish display of service to others.

Special Olympics is big in the South. Unlike Ohio, Alabama's Special Olympics program was school-based, making it convenient for Greg to participate. He and other students qualified for the state meet, held at Auburn University. The meet took place on a late spring Saturday, but it was really a full weekend event for Greg and the other athletes. They took a school bus to Auburn after class on Friday. They stayed in the college dorm rooms. On Saturday evening, after the meet, they had a dance in the gym. The bus brought them back home on Sunday morning.

As for the meet, Greg was the state champion in his age group for the softball throw. In the spirit of full disclosure, he was the only participant in his age group for that event. He also did the 100-meter dash. But he didn't dash, he loped. I stood near the track and tried to spur him on, "Go, Greg!" This had the opposite of its intended effect, as he slowed and looked in my direction – trying to understand where that familiar voice was coming from and why it was at top volume.

The great thing about our Alabama experience: We met lots of new people. We bonded with two other families in our neighborhood who had children with disabilities. A couple of local college students were Greg's caregivers. Anne's new friends accepted him with open arms. Best of all, Greg's heart was blessed hundreds of times. If you've spent any time in the South, you know that anyone who experiences a hardship or challenge often gets a friendly reference, "Bless his heart."

When it came time to return to Ohio, Greg received a picture album from his schoolmates. His teacher wrote a nice farewell note in the album:

> *Greg, we will miss you so much. It won't be the same without you! I will miss your sweet smile and humor. And I'll really miss my "Diet Coke" buddy. Take care and good luck at your new school.*

We've had a few negative experiences in the community. The most recent happened not so long ago in Ohio.

Greg enjoys going to bookstores. He'll first peruse the DVDs, looking especially for the latest *Sesame Street* or Christmas offerings. He'll move on to the picture books in the children's section. We'll also treat him to a snack at the coffee shop. When we exit the car in the parking lot of the bookstore, he has a spring in his step. His pace picks up as we near the door. Think of how you feel when you're about to get started on one of your favorite activities.

Greg was at the store's entry door, a few steps ahead of me. He's learned to say "excuse me" if he's passing close to someone. On this day, he didn't say it. A grandmotherly woman happened to be approaching the door at the same time. Greg brushed past her, eager to get to the DVD racks. She scowled at his back and then said in my direction, "Well, young man, I guess your mother never taught you any manners!" I gave her an apology and explained, with sharpness in my voice, that he had autism and really didn't know any better. I was steaming that she had dissed both my son and my wife. If I had better presence of mind, I would have said to her, "By the way, his mother has taught him well. She doesn't need you to be judging her parenting skills. She could probably educate you to Greg's challenge."

Incidents like that are few. People are understanding, including the cashiers at the grocery store or gas station. Greg is particular about bags and receipts. If we're just buying a candy bar, he wants it in a bag with a receipt. When the transaction is complete, he'll often want to shake the cashier's hand – a social skill taught to him at school. He'll hold out his hand until the cashier shakes it. I enjoy watching the looks on their faces. Surprise turns to wariness to friendliness in milliseconds. When we happen upon the same cashier a second or third time, they'll whisper to me, "I really enjoy seeing him."

Our neighborhood grocery stores have attended play areas for young children. These areas have shelves of children's

DVDs, including *Sesame Street* and Christmas movies. We don't let Greg go into the play areas, but we do let him peer over the counter. He points out his favorite movies on the shelves. The play area workers know him well. They just smile, amused by his ritual.

Greg's first haircut set the stage for a lifelong friendship. When he was very young, he was tactilely defensive. We had no confidence that he'd sit through the process of a haircut. I shirked my parental responsibilities here, not wanting to be the one who gave him a bad haircut or, worse yet, gouged his ear. So the mop on his head continued to grow and grow. Something had to be done.

Doreen to the rescue, another flash of brilliance. As naptime approached, she loaded him into his car seat and took a drive, knowing that he'd fall asleep in the seat. She pulled up to the curb in front of the salon, and begged Karen to come out to the car with her scissors and comb. Greg slept through his first trim.

This wasn't a long-term solution. Before long, we coaxed him into the salon. Karen had moved on, so Laurie became his haircut provider. At first, we employed the "non-stop distractions" method. We'd feed him his favorite candy and help him do sticker books while Laurie worked frantically. I held his head in place during the delicate parts of the process. To Laurie's credit, we never had the slightest injury, not to mention the professional quality of her work.

Greg grew accustomed to the haircut ritual, becoming self-sufficient – no need for distractions. He had no trouble adapting to a new haircutter during his years in Alabama.

Returning to Ohio, we returned to Laurie. Now, Greg walks into the salon like he owns the place. The owner and staff know him well. He's got a routine that includes a trip to the water cooler and a test of the old-fashioned hooded hair dryers. He's got an exemption from the "no spinning in the chair" rule. His ritual is to give himself two spins, 360 degrees in each direction. He's knowledgeable about all of the elements of the service he receives. If they forget something, he'll remind them. Laurie once forgot to put powder on his neck at the end of the haircut. Greg spoke up, "Powder?" When the cut is finished, if the receptionist doesn't produce the basket of lollipops, he'll go behind the counter and get it himself.

He can generalize these skills. He goes to the dentist twice yearly for a cleaning. He understands the process, and he's a good patient. The same applies to doctor visits, though Greg will bargain for "no needle" when we're en route to the doctor's office. He doesn't always get his wish. He needs the occasional TB test or flu shot.

Years ago, he was terrified of that part of doctor visits. Three or four people had to hold him so the nurse could give him the shot. These days, those moments are still very hard for him. Though his heart races, he does sit still and endure the needle trauma. This progress might seem insignificant to most parents. Doreen swells with pride when she sees her 23-year-old son's bravery.

Back to Laurie. From the time she met Greg, she was interested in him and in his progress. She'd ask questions. She became an armchair expert in child development, and she passed on advice to new parents among her family, clients and co-workers. She's observed Greg's progress from toddler to adult. She's always accepted him, no matter what behavior was on display.

She even invited him to her wedding. He and I went and got an aisle seat at the ceremony. As Laurie came down the aisle, Greg reached out and gave her a high five. Another priceless moment.

I don't think that Greg always feels the warmth of the community. We do. As Ms. Kingsley wrote, "You will meet a whole new group of people you would never have met."

Chapter 9: How Healthy Are You My Mother?

How to explain my son, twenty-three years into this journey? The boy who ransacked his bedroom, went through a phase of self-injury, whose interests have ebbed and flowed. The boy with an encyclopedic list of dates and personal events in his head, neatly stored, uncluttered by worries of responsibility, social acceptance, and the subconscious fears that plague the rest of us.

He's happy. Really happy. Satisfied, comfortable with his life. He enjoys the moment. Enjoys most of his moments. He still gets frustrated from time to time. But he can get past the frustration, usually within 30 minutes. He doesn't worry about the next day, next week, or next year, except to understand what events and activities are scheduled. Once the event is on the calendar, he can wait patiently for an hour, a week, or a year. He's unencumbered. He's free.

He's funny. Funny, humorous. Funny, unique. He's fun to be around. Where'd he get his sense of humor? I suppose all of us in the family are partly responsible.

Greg's brand of humor? Opposites and absurdities. One of his lines to draw a reaction from me and get himself laughing: "Sleep in day, wake up at night?" When we approach our car in a parking lot, he'll point to another nearby car and say, "Greg is sitting in the red truck?" He'll also speak about a past event in the present tense, knowing that what he did was wrong when it happened. "Greg is dumping purple medicine in the sink?" "Greg is spilling oatmeal at preschool?"

From a young age, he was interested in children's books. Mercer Mayer's *Little Critter* series. Stan and Jan's *Berenstain Bears*. Dr. Seuss books, including the classic written by Seuss's alter ego, Theo LeSieg: *Wacky Wednesday*.

Academic testing shows that Greg reads at a second-grade level, struggling to comprehend written material. Yet, he has practically memorized hundreds of children's books that consist of great picture art with a few explanatory words per page. Those books, taken all together, represent a do-it-yourself guide to living. Even though he doesn't look at the books much anymore, they sit on the shelves in his bedroom. He knows how to find each one. When it's time to go to the dentist, he'll run upstairs to retrieve Mercer Mayer's *Just Going to the Dentist*. This is his roadmap, a way to help him make sense of the world.

The books also explain a joke of his. He came up to me and said, "How healthy are you my mother?" Then he laughed. I figured out this was his play on words. At school, he was learning about nutrition. They were trying to teach him to read food labels. There must have been a poster or some class material that asked the question, "How healthy are you?" Greg put that together with P.D. Eastman's book *Are You My Mother?*. The result is a sophisticated form of humor.

The latest, most interesting window to Greg's mind comes courtesy of the invention of satellite radio. We have it in our car. He enjoys reading the display screen as we ride, relating the information on the screen to things in his life.

Here's an example of the display screen format and content:

CHANNEL	**016 The Blend**
CATEGORY	**Pop**
NAME	**Rod Stewart**
TITLE	**Maggie May**

Greg's comment about this one: "Pretzel rod. Fishing rod."

NAME	**Toto**
TITLE	**Africa**

Greg: "Toto in the bathroom." (He's seen the Toto brand on bathroom fixtures.)

NAME	**Laura Branigan**
TITLE	**Gloria**

Greg: "Gloria in church." (We're Catholic; the Gloria is part of the Mass.)

The display has room for only 16 characters per line. This causes Greg to have to improvise.

NAME	**REO Speedwagon**
TITLE	**Can't Fight This**

Greg: "Daddy help?" [Translation: "Dad, what are the rest of the words in the song title?"]

Me: "Can't fight this feeling."

Greg: "Feeling better."

NAME **B.J. Thomas**
TITLE **Hooked On A Feel**

Greg: "Fish hook. Feeling better."

He'll add letters or words even when they're not required. Because the concept as displayed means little to him:

NAME **Paul McCartney**
TITLE **Live and Let Die**

Greg: "Live and Let Diet Coke."

NAME **Beyonce**
TITLE **Ave Maria**

Greg: "Avenue Maria."

NAME **AC/DC**
TITLE **Highway to Hell**

Greg: "Highway to hello."

Besides pretzel rods, other food references are favorites for him:

NAME **Fleetwood Mac**
TITLE **Sara**

Greg: "Fleetwood mac and cheese."

NAME **John Mayer**
TITLE **Say**

Greg: "Oscar Mayer hot dog."

He's become a music aficionado. Often, I'll have the car radio tuned to the Seventies channel. Our current next-door neighbors have the last name Greene. A while ago, Greg and I returned home in our car. As we pulled into our driveway, Greg pointed to the house next door and said, "Al Green's house." Problem is, our neighbor's first name is Steve. I later told Steve that Greg had changed his name to Al. I also asked if he could brush up on the lyrics to *Let's Stay Together*.

Greg will also comment on background music. He and I went for a haircut. He went first, and then sat in the waiting area while Laurie cut my hair. The salon was busy that day. Between the conversations, the hair dryers and other noise, I couldn't hear the background music. But Greg could filter it through. He got up from the waiting area and approached Laurie and me. He said, "Daddy help. Spell it soak." I had no idea why he wanted me to confirm for him how to spell the word "soak." When I told him, he said, "Soak up the sun." Only then could I faintly hear Sheryl Crow's song playing in the background.

Greg loves Christmas, and a Christmas song was at the bottom of a mystery that took us months to solve. We noticed that when we were driving around town, Greg would mutter to himself, "A moment." None of us could figure it out. He didn't say the phrase every time we passed a certain landmark. He seemed to say it randomly. We had no idea why he said it.

He finally let me in on the secret. I was driving on the freeway, with Greg in the front passenger seat. Just the two of us, cruising across town. He said that phrase again, "A moment." I quizzed him, "Greg, what is 'a moment'?" He replied, "They only paused a moment when they heard him holler, 'Stop'!"

I looked in the rearview mirror; saw that a police cruiser had stopped a motorist. The cruiser's lights were flashing. Greg had been saying "a moment" every time we passed a police car stopped with its lights flashing. When you've watched the *Frosty the Snowman* video as much as we have, you know that there's a police officer with a whistle who stops the traffic so that Frosty and the kids can cross the street.

Greg navigates the internet. His favorite sites are YouTube for videos, Amazon and eBay for books and movies, and the *Sesame Street* website for clips of old skits. He knows how to enter his search criteria. He'll click the links to bring up what he wants to see. Fortunately, he doesn't understand the concept of a credit card, so he can't make purchases while he surfs.

He gets his Christmas fix on these websites. One day, I came into our computer room to find him watching the *Frosty the Snowman* video on YouTube. The video was some kind of off-color parody. The images were from the original Frosty cartoon, but some YouTuber had inserted a not-so-nice soundtrack. I walked in, heard a gruff voice saying something like, "Yeah, I'm f***ing Frosty the Snowman and you can kiss my a**!" Greg's face showed no reaction.

One of my favorite pictures. At the end of a summer shower ... Greg was fascinated with the view and the sounds under that umbrella.

“Sledding” on a piece of cardboard. Greg liked the snow, and he liked to go fast.

Computer literate at a very young age. Here he follows along as the program reads a book to him.

A very active and normal-looking boy.

Haircuts were an adventure when Greg was young. Here the "mop" isn't too bad – must've had a recent trim.

Class picture 1993-94. The teacher keeps a gentle, but firm hold on Greg ... to keep him from running off.

Greg's bedroom after a "nap" ... at age two.

Seventh birthday party at Chuck E. Cheese. Our neighbor Jane made Greg a life-size Guy Smiley. He loved it.

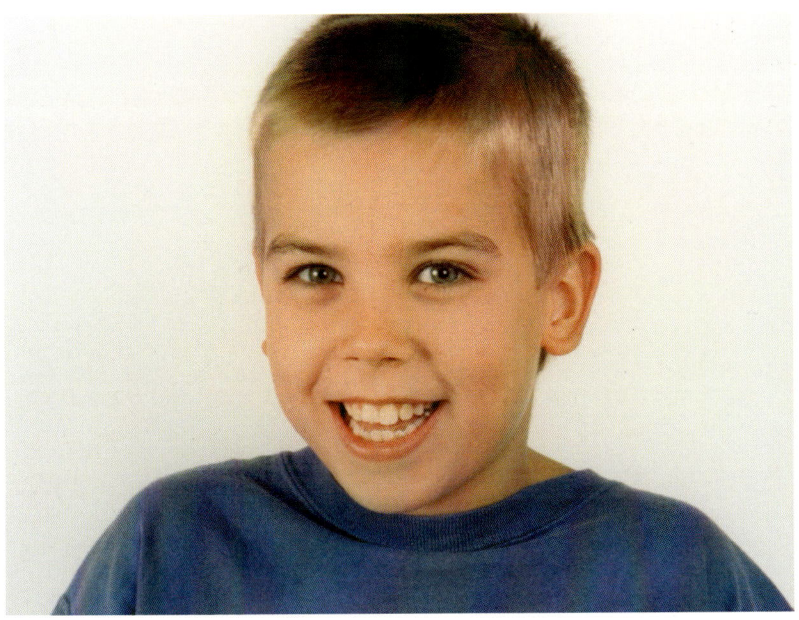

Cute kid. Don't be fooled ... he could cause a lot of mischief.

Greg's freehand drawing of the stage at Chuck E. Cheese, circa 1995. Amazing detail.

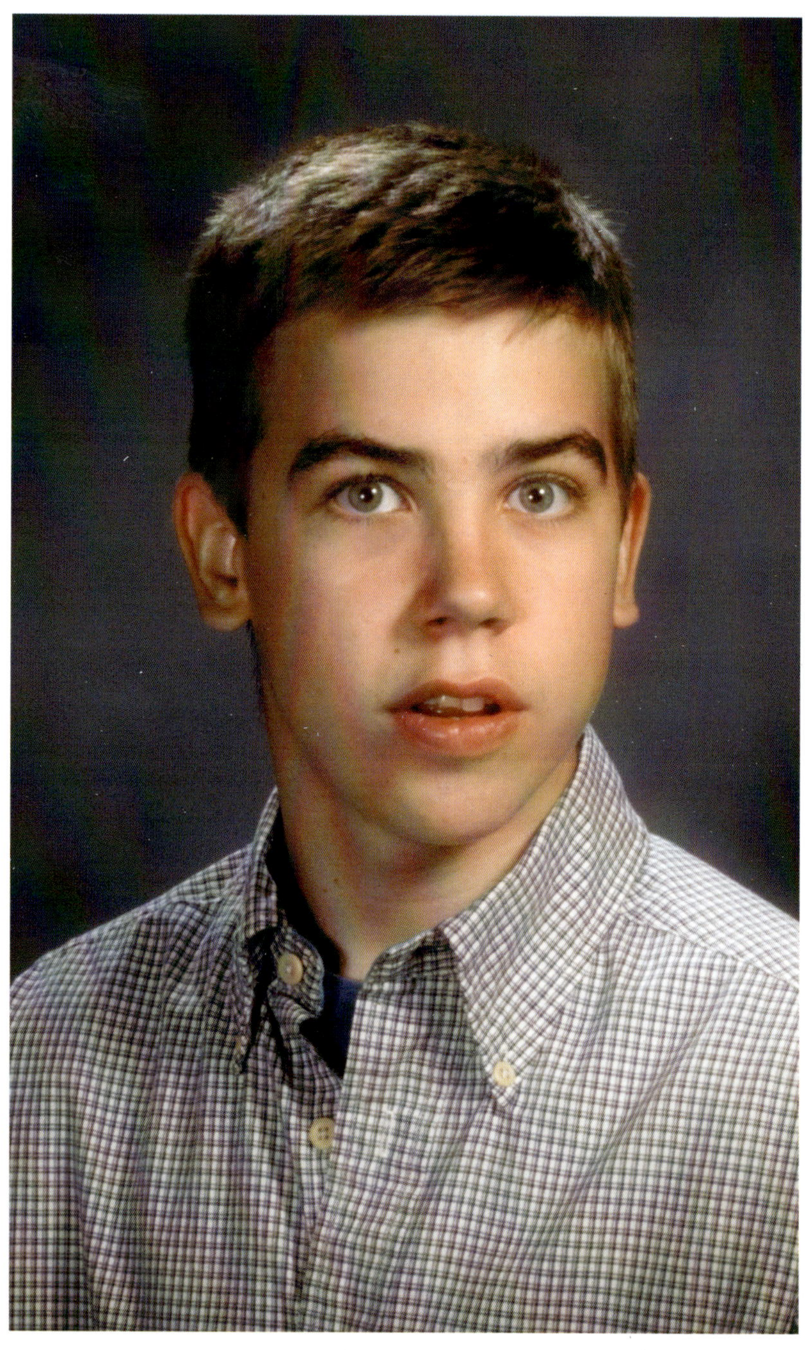

A school picture in the adolescent years. Hard to get a good school picture at this age.

Fall 2010. Greg and Anne. Brother and sister. No sibling rivalry here.

"Telephone banana?" Enjoying his own joke.

Greg and The Godfather, Mr. Shelley Stewart.

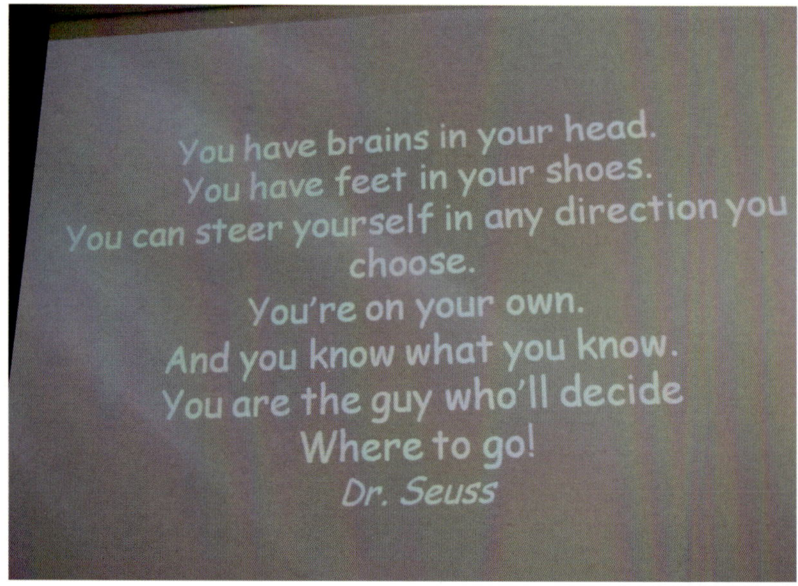

Greg's speech at the Project Search graduation in 2010.

Greg reading his graduation speech.

Graduation. Who'd have believed it? Anne helped her brother strike this pose.

He watched the video as if nothing were amiss. I prompted him to move along to the next video link, thankful there are things that go over his head.

Greg is calendar and time oriented. Obsessed. He looks for repetition – daily, monthly, annually. If we take a trip to Chicago in April, he'll assume that we'll go back to the same place in April of the following year. We've enjoyed some benefits because of this trait. For Greg, bedtime is bedtime, so he rarely gives us any flak about that. The downside is he'll get upset if we're running late or miss a scheduled activity.

Greg is a world-class Word Searcher. He enjoys passing time with paperback books of those puzzles where words are hidden backwards, forwards, down, up and diagonally in a grid. The hidden words are listed beside the grid, usually in alphabetical order. Greg's approach to these puzzles is the polar opposite of mine, ten times more effective.

I glance through the list of words and study the grid to see if a word pops out for me. When it does, I'll circle it in the puzzle and cross it off the list. My speed increases just slightly when I've got several words circled on the grid; the remaining hidden words are a little more visible.

Greg does the words in order. He'll cross the first word off the list, then look at the grid and circle the word. He finds it almost immediately because his vision is so acute. He moves on to the next word on the list. Works at a steady pace, finishing the puzzle in a fraction of the time it takes me. One time he couldn't find a word in the grid. As it turned out, there was a misprint. The word on the list was not in the grid.

This skill also applies to jigsaw puzzles. He's quick. I finally learned his secret. He pays no attention to the picture on the puzzle box or to the faces of the puzzle pieces. He fits the pieces together by shape alone. I'd have a headache if I tried that.

In his down time, Greg is a babbler. His consciousness wanders off, and he talks to himself. He has an endless supply of recorded material in his brain. His babbling monologues have structure and typically feature lots of repetition. He talks fast, so it's hard to understand what he's saying. If we listen closely, we can hear snippets of familiar things — a *Sesame Street* skit or a few lines from a book. These are mixed in with other content that only makes sense to Greg. He delivers these lines in a singsong, high-pitched voice.

Greg is intensely private about these babblings. If we interrupt him or make some comment about what he's saying, he'll reply, "Greg is happy." Translation: "I'm doing just fine. What I'm talking about is my business. How about you leave me alone and let me do my thing?"

Greg is affectionate with his closest family members. He'll nuzzle close to us on the couch. If we ask, he'll give hugs and kisses. He wants to keep track of each of us. His sister lives on Ohio State's campus. Greg has been there, so he has a visual of where she is. But once or twice a day, he'll ask me or Doreen about her. It's a very brief conversation. Greg will say, "Annie?" We'll say, "She's at OSU." He wants to be reassured about her status. He does the same thing to keep track of his father and mother if we're out of the house for an extended period.

Anne was watching her brother one day while we were out. Greg asked about Mom and Dad. Anne said, "They're gone." When his eyes widened, Anne realized her mistake. (Grandpa died, he's gone ...) She quickly clarified that we weren't gone forever, that we'd be back.

Greg lives a well-ordered and predictable life. He enjoys being out and about, taking in the audio and visual stimulation of the world around him. He can communicate sufficiently well to get along without our help. He understands that things can change, and he has the ability to adapt. I've known him since his birth, and I have him 99.9% figured out. There's just one mystery I can't solve.

As background, Greg has a very high tolerance for pain. He doesn't cry when he gets hurt. Now and then, he'll cry for no apparent reason. This has happened four times I can remember. Once, we were in the car, near the end of a two-hour trip to visit relatives. Another time, we were at his grandparents' house. The third and fourth times, we were at home. His eyes well with tears, and he sobs deeply. When we try to comfort him, to ask what's the matter, he simply says, "Greg is sad, is crying." We're unable to get him to explain why he's sad.

What's going on in his head at these times? It goes against everything I know about him. If he wants something, he asks for it. He can usually accept the answer "no." His emotions are easy to interpret. There is no nuance with him; he doesn't act or put up a front. He's inwardly focused. His brain's wiring doesn't allow him to put himself in another's shoes. That's our son. We know him better than anyone. So why does he have these episodes of sadness? I suppose we'll never know.

Chapter 10: Graduation

Nearing the end of Greg's school eligibility, the focus turned to vocational preparation. In his second-to-last year, he was in a program outside a traditional school setting. He and seven other students were housed in a small office building in the community. From there, they were taken to local work sites. They spent several hours a day in work training, with teachers and aides available as job coaches. They'd go back to their "classroom" before the end of the day to continue learning vocational and life skills.

Another exciting opportunity came as Greg approached his final year of school eligibility. Our Dublin high schools partnered with a neighboring school district and a nearby technical school, launching a program called Project Search. The program, based at a local hospital, would be open to about ten special education students in their last year of school. The students would spend their entire school year at the hospital as interns. All day, every school day. The interns would have a home base in a small hospital conference room. They'd rotate through nine-week job assignments. The goal was employment, at either the hospital or elsewhere in the community. It was great to have the hospital, a private employer in the community, collaborate with local schools to provide this opportunity.

Admission to the program was competitive. More students applied than could be accommodated. Though it sounded like a wonderful opportunity, we weren't very optimistic about Greg's chances. There would be selection interviews. With Greg's weakness in communication, we couldn't see him standing out. We almost didn't have him apply for the program. In the end, we reasoned that the school district was trying something new, and we ought to support their initiative by participating. We had a good backup plan: the same community-centered program he was in the previous year, during which he made excellent progress. So we signed him up, and all the students were invited to Interview Day.

The day started with a general session. School and hospital personnel explained the program to a roomful of students and parents. Then they asked the parents to leave the room so that they could conduct the interviews. Two students sat at each table, across from the interviewers, who were school and hospital staff.

During the general information session, Greg was well behaved but not particularly attentive. Despite our attempts to prepare him, I doubt that he could understand the presentations that were being made. When it came time for us to leave the room and let the interviews begin, I was worried. Greg had none of my nervousness. I talked to him for a minute, told him to sit up straight, fold his hands and rest them on the table. Then we left the room. As I got to the doorway on my way out, I snuck a look back at him. He was scratching an itch on his cheek. But he was doing it with his hands still folded! My son can follow instructions.

About 30 minutes later, the parents came back into the room. Greg was sitting in his chair, his hands still folded on the table. It turned out that the interview went pretty well. His teacher had prepared a binder for him that included pictures of Greg doing various jobs in the community. A visual resume. The hospital staff person was able to converse with him, using the pictures as a reference. With the help of the school district's transition coordinator, Greg got across the key points about his work skills and experiences.

A few days later, we were notified that Greg had been accepted into the new program for the next school year. To think we almost didn't have him apply! It was another important lesson: never underestimate what he can do.

Knowing that Greg's days in a school setting were over, we decided to have him graduate before he started the hospital-based program. If we waited a year, there would be fewer peer and teacher connections to Greg. The term for it is "social graduation" — donning a cap and gown, walking the stage, but not receiving a diploma.

Greg was assigned a non-graduating peer buddy to sit with him to make sure he got through the ceremony. That day was special for us. Greg was 21, three years older than the other graduates, and we were celebrating not just his years in a high school placement, but the entirety of his schooling, which covered 18 years. During her speech, the school principal made a point of acknowledging Greg and another special needs student who sat among the graduates. When it came time to line up and walk across the stage, Greg was nonchalant. I was just the opposite. This was the third time I cried. This time, the emotions were pride and joy. I had in my mind's eye all of the class pictures, starting from preschool. I knew well the long route he had taken, the effort he had expended, the progress he had made against strong odds.

We threw a party for him the next day. He had turned 21 several months before, and for that occasion, we'd invited extended family members. The same approach didn't feel right for his graduation party. This was the end of a long school journey, one he couldn't have completed successfully if not for the support of scores of people: teachers, aides, therapists, school administrators, bus drivers, camp counselors, and so many others. We wanted the focus to be on Greg and the school staff who had helped him through.

We thought all the way back to his preschool days, listed up the school personnel to invite. Some we hadn't seen or heard from in more than 15 years. We plumbed our network of contacts, got on whitepages.com, and tried to find them. We succeeded in finding contact information for several of them, and many whom we invited were gracious enough to attend. Some had retired. Others were in new careers, like a former teacher's aide who'd become a police officer. Immediate family members rounded out the crowd.

It was a gloriously sunny late May day, adding to a very special celebration. Reminiscence was in the air, and the time passed much too quickly. The best moments were watching Greg reunite with people he hadn't seen in many years. Of course, Greg had changed — he'd grown up. But he was still easily recognizable to them. In reality, their appearance had changed much more than Greg's. When we told Greg who they were, he gave them a quick once-over and made the connection. Soon he was reciting the school year and school building where he had known them. Then, he'd mention an experience the two of them had shared. At that point, the real story was in their faces: a look that said, "He remembers me! He appreciates the time we spent together."

We purchased a guest book, the kind you might see at a wedding or other event. We encouraged our guests to write a note to Greg. This sampling of quotes is a testament to the way he enriched their lives:

> *"The best memory was helping him learn to read, know the calendar and help him count his lunch money."*

> *"I feel very lucky to have been your teacher. You always put a smile on my face. I am so proud of you."*

> *"I'm so proud of you and what you accomplished. I really miss your expertise at trimming laminated items."*

> *"I'll never forget you. You've come so far and have done such a great job. I'm so proud of you."*

> *"From the first time I saw you, I loved you. You are such a sweet boy. Love ya!"*

The graduation was step one of the transition process. One more school year in the hospital intern program lay ahead. Beyond that would be the real transition.

Part 3

ASD In Our Society

Autism is mysterious and confounding.
How is it caused? How should it be treated?
There are no black-and-white answers.

Chapter 11: The Cause Debate

Throughout the years, we haven't spent a lot of time trying to figure out how or why autism found Greg. At a support group meeting we attended soon after Greg was diagnosed, an experienced parent said about the cause of autism: "What does it matter?" That statement may seem narrow-minded or even cruel. But it's very pragmatic. In effect, this was his advice:

> *You only have so much time and energy. You can spend your time looking backward, asking why, blaming yourself or blaming someone else. At the end of the day, your child won't receive much benefit from that effort. Far better to spend your energy handling the current situation and planning for the future.*

It's human nature to look back. Doreen had a 36-hour labor giving birth to Greg. To help the labor progress, she was given the drug Pitocin intravenously. We've wondered if the lengthy labor, the drug or two hours of pushing had anything to do with Greg's condition. We've thought about a possible environmental connection. A childhood friend of mine (we grew up on the same street) has a son with

Asperger's Syndrome. We've considered genetics. When I stop to analyze my own traits, I have to admit that some of them tend toward those of a person with ASD. For example, I can easily eat the same thing for lunch every weekday. It seems to me that genetics might explain why autism is four times more common for males than females. We've also thought about the mental health issues of some of our ancestors. Finally, we've thought about external factors like the measles, mumps and rubella (MMR) vaccine.

My own guess is genetics. That's certainly something I'll never prove, but it does beg a question that parents of children with ASD face: If autism is genetic, and it's more likely that you'll have another child with ASD, does that affect your thinking about having more children?

In our case, that question was moot. Greg and Anne are only 22 months apart. She was conceived before we had concerns about Greg's development, and she was born before we had a diagnosis. We never talked seriously about having a third child. Our plan was to have two children. We figured that having only two would allow us to play "man-to-man," not have to go to a zone defense. The challenge of Greg's autism helped cement our "two and through" decision.

Doreen sometimes wishes that we'd had a third child. Thinking that another sibling would have been good for Anne. Would have given her a confidante, someone to share her feelings and burdens.

It's incredibly important to find the cause of autism. That's the only way the incidence rate can flatten, decline and ultimately approach zero. In hopes of that outcome, I'm a strong advocate for autism research. I'm also a realist. Even if there is a lot of progress in the next 10 or 20 years, the prospects for a cure are slim for Greg and many others like him. Brings me back to the advice we got years ago. On a purely individual level, "What does it matter?" Greg has autism. He's in his early 20s. What are we going to do to support him going forward?

I want to touch on the vaccine issue. A very emotional topic for the last decade or so. An ongoing battle between parents and some researchers on one side, doctors and drug makers on the other. Add a supporting cast of politicians, lawyers, academics and media.

As with Greg, autism often manifests in the child's second year. Since vaccines are first administered early in a child's life, it's logical to look for a connection. At first, the culprit was thought to be a small amount of mercury that was used as a preservative in vaccines. By 2001, the mercury had been removed from children's vaccines. Some still question the number of vaccines being administered in a short period of time. There are still many people who believe that vaccines cause or contribute to autism.

I suppose there are two primary motivations for parents of children with ASD to fight this battle. One of those motivations is absolutely on the mark. The other is less clear.

The first motivation is simple. Make sure that the vaccines

are safe. I think that's been accomplished. In a societal sense, we must acknowledge the benefits gained from the vaccines: the eradication of diseases that had widespread effects years ago.

The second motivation might sound simple, but far from it. We want justice. Said another way, "You did this to my child and you should bear the consequences." This satisfies the human desire for fairness. Some entity and/or some people should pay for the trouble they caused. There should be some restitution.

The legal process moves slowly. Even if you accept that vaccines were part of the cause, what's the remedy? How do you calculate the damages? What amount equals the lifetime of resources needed to support a person with ASD? Those questions have been answered recently.

The federal government has set up a vaccine court to hear claims. Last time I checked, there were about 5,000 cases pending. One case was settled in 2010. That family was awarded $1.5 million, plus $500,000 annually for the rest of the child's life. The settlement in that case has a net present value of about $20 million.

If each of the 5,000 pending cases had the same result, the total would be $100 billion. That's 2.5 times BP's estimated oil spill liability. The result of this theoretical scenario? A tiny fraction of people with ASD would receive financial support. There would be insolvent pharmaceutical and insurance companies. And well-enriched trial lawyers.

Don't get me wrong. I support our justice system and the right of every person to have their claim adjudicated. Just don't confuse individual legal case results with solutions to a problem that's affecting one of every 110 people born today.

In early 2009, *Newsweek* published an article about an executive who resigned from an autism-related non-profit organization over the vaccine issue. Her point: It's wasteful to continue research into the vaccine-autism link. "We have very limited resources and every dollar we spend looking where we know the answer isn't is a dollar we don't have to spend where we might actually find new answers."

There's one area where the ASD community is united. We all feel the frustration of not knowing the cause. Research must continue, must accelerate. There are a lot of people with ASD who need help.

Chapter 12: Treatment Approaches

During the childhood of a person with ASD, the family meets the basic needs of food, shelter, clothing, safety and security. The family provides healthcare, through employer-based or individually purchased medical insurance policies. The family's circumstances determine whether they are eligible for other government programs to supplement income and health care. Education services are the responsibility of the local public schools. The basic needs of children with ASD are provided for.

The biggest variable in the support of a young child with ASD is additional treatment and support. We're talking about treatments provided outside of the school setting. This wild card tends to overlap the educational and medical service areas.

Treatment approaches have evolved in my son's lifetime. When Greg was diagnosed in 1990, Applied Behavioral Analysis (ABA) was new and subject to controversy. What is ABA? It's an individualized program for children with ASD to improve on any kind of skill, hopefully lessening the effects of autism. It involves intensive, repetitive training coupled with a structured system of immediate reward for improvements.

In the early 1990s, depending on whom you asked, Professor O. Ivar Lovaas, an ABA pioneer at UCLA, was either a dangerous crackpot or a wonderful innovator. ABA was available only in certain regions of the country. We remember hearing about ABA experts in California and at Vanderbilt in Tennessee. As the years went by, it became more widely accepted and used.

That presents Doreen and me with a chance to take a stroll down Guilty Lane. We didn't provide ABA services for Greg. We can look back over the last 20 years and play "Woulda-Coulda-Shoulda."

What did we do for him? When we first got the diagnosis, we went into a frenzy. The internet wasn't much back then, so we used "old school" methods like going to the library, making phone calls and joining a support group. We were willing to try almost anything. We had many consults with speech therapists, psychologists and other professionals. One meeting with a psychologist was going well until Greg picked up a glass of water and dumped it on the good doctor. Greg still talks about that, "Greg is spilling water man has blue shirt."

We gave Greg a vitamin B-12 supplement. We tried a tactile stimulation method of brushing his skin. These and other approaches were short-term – we didn't see results. We got him additional speech therapy outside of the school setting for about five years. We tried to find medications to improve some of the behaviors that hindered his development. Mainly aggression and difficulty falling asleep. By the age of ten, his behavior moderated. We stopped searching for treatments, relying instead on the public school system, summer camps, caregivers and our own efforts to help maximize his capability.

Do Doreen and I second-guess ourselves? Do we regret not providing Greg ABA therapy upon diagnosis, when he was a preschooler? No. We sleep each night with a clear conscience. We won't walk down Guilty Lane.

Nonetheless, I know that things would be different if Greg were born today. We would do ABA. The topic of therapy is a big issue for the parents of kids now being diagnosed. There's broad agreement on the value of early intervention – identifying the concern areas and accessing services right away. Upon diagnosis, the child often being age two or three, today's parents are counseled to get the child into ABA or something like it. It's not unusual for therapy to be recommended for four hours per day after school days and eight hours per day on weekends. Eight hours also during summer and other school breaks. That's more than 40 hours a week on average. At $15/hour for therapists' time, more than $30,000 a year.

How does that $30,000 get paid? Although it's the exception rather than the rule, some health insurance policies cover a portion of the cost. A handful of states have passed healthcare mandates for autism therapies. The 2010 federal healthcare reform legislation will require the government-organized exchange plans to cover evidence-based therapies up to $36,000 per year, beginning in 2014. Another funding source is through government programs, notably Medicaid waivers. Without insurance coverage or a Medicaid waiver, a family is on its own. We know families who paid the full cost out of their own pocket. That's a financial hardship, no matter what your socioeconomic status.

With the skyrocketing incidence rate and the trend toward intensive therapy at a very early age, there are huge dollars going toward this treatment approach. There's an industry that's grown up around ABA. Lots of consultants. Many different providers of services. I'm sure that the vast majority of them have the best interest of the children with ASD and their families at heart. It does worry me a bit: $30,000 per person per year gets the attention of capitalists.

If Greg were a toddler today, he'd probably be getting ABA therapy. But I think there's a danger in having ABA as the exclusive treatment. The child ends up spending hundreds of hours in one-on-one therapy, in a home or office setting. Not much time left for getting out, for living life in the community. The world is a strange place for people with ASD. The best way for them to learn to get along is through experience. ABA wouldn't have taught Greg how to behave at McDonald's. Through repeated experiences, we got him to learn that it wasn't cool to walk over to another table and sample their food.

Today, ABA or similar therapies are the predominant treatment methods. How's it going so far? What are the long-term prospects for these kids? Will they be able to live with more independence as adults?

Nobody really knows. While children with ASD have common traits, they are all unique. What works for some doesn't work for others. We know several families with children younger than Greg who have tried intensive therapy. We're not aware of any miracle cures.

Looking at the big picture, where do we go from here? No simple answer. There are three high priority areas:

> 1. ***Research.***
> Find the cause(s) and improve the medical and pharmacological treatments.
>
> 2. ***Early Diagnosis and Intervention.***
> If the best chance for improvement is in those early years, we can't let them go to waste.
>
> 3. ***Special Education.***
> We have a good educational system. It's individualized. We can adapt the curriculum and the services with the goal of increasing cognitive and functional skills.

I can't see anything to counteract the increase in the number of adults with ASD. In fifteen years, there will be thousands upon thousands of young adults with ASD in Greg's same situation: exiting the protection of our public education system and entering the world of adult services. A world that they're likely to remain a part of for another 60+ years. How will we support them?

Chapter 13: Other Perspectives

My perspective is from the middle of the autism spectrum. There's a lot I don't know about the two ends of the spectrum. This was made clear to me at a recent event.

We attended an autism walk, a fundraiser for an autism-related organization. The event was held on Ohio State University's campus. Toward the end of the walk, we encountered a small group of protesters at the curbside. Their posters read, "We Can Speak for Ourselves" and "I'm a Person, Not a Puzzle Piece."

I took this to be a group of individuals on the spectrum, obviously with good communication skills. It's possible that many of them had the Asperger's diagnosis. I was surprised to see a protest at an autism charity event. Once I processed the information, my reaction was positive. I'll almost always support free speech and self-expression.

There may be a growing trend for the Asperger's community to break away from the ASD crowd. Some people with Asperger's attend college. Some get married and have families. Adults with Asperger's don't face all of the transition issues that Greg is facing. They do face their own unique issues.

In early childhood, the educational and treatment approaches may be similar for people with Asperger's and others on the autism spectrum. The difference widens as these groups age. It's understandable that adults with Asperger's want to speak for themselves.

My sense is that a good amount of the increase in the ASD incidence rate has come from people on the higher-functioning end of the spectrum. I have no data to support this. But I'm seeing more and more stories about adults just recently diagnosed. Invariably, their social and communication skills are far advanced, compared to my son.

Another group outside of my experience are those more profoundly affected. Those whose communication is extremely limited. Those with one or more conditions in addition to autism. They have an even higher mountain to climb to realize some level of inclusion in the community as adults.

This more profoundly affected group is often the source of great breakthroughs. When finding the right communication device unlocks the door, and we find a highly intelligent person with much to say and contribute. When a talent for singing or art is discovered. When an odd skill or interest can be parlayed into a productive activity, even an occupation.

At the end of the day, it makes no difference whether we continue to work on behalf of one group, or a couple of subgroups. All people with ASD need advocates.

Part 4

Transition to Adulthood
So Far, So Good

The pieces begin to fall into place,
but there's one big unknown.

Chapter 14: Early Transition Steps

I'm sounding like an old man when I say that the time has passed quickly. It seems a short time ago that Greg went off to preschool.

We kept him in a school placement through age 22, using the last eight years to focus on vocational and functional life skills. This delayed his transition by about four years compared to exiting school as a typical high school senior at age 18.

With prompting from school administrators and our case manager, we thought about transition for several years. As Greg neared the end of his school eligibility, we took care of four early transition steps: guardianship, SSI, a special needs trust and a Medicaid waiver.

Guardianship

In Ohio and 46 other states, the age of majority is 18. Alabama is 19. At this age, a person is no longer a minor in the eyes of the law. A parent's legal responsibility and legal control end here.

Since the capabilities of people with ASD vary across the spectrum, there's no standard answer what to do about guardianship when the child reaches legal adulthood. Some people with ASD may be capable of making their own decisions. Others have limited or no skills for making judgments. In Greg's case, Doreen and I thought it best to maintain legal control, so we applied to our local probate court to be appointed as his co-guardians.

The person who has a guardian is referred to as the ward. There are two aspects of guardianship. A "guardian of the person" ensures that life decisions are made in the ward's best interest. A "guardian of the estate" oversees the ward's resources (money). The same person can serve as the guardian of the person and guardian of the estate.

It's important to understand two things about guardianships. First, it's equivalent to having your adult child declared legally incompetent. For some parents, that's a big and scary step. Second, the legal process to become the guardian of your adult child is, in a sense, adversarial. The judge considers the adult child independent from the parents. The court will likely appoint an attorney or other professional to represent the child during the guardianship proceedings. In this way, the court can be assured that the wishes of the child are taken into account.

In our case, the court appointed a representative to independently verify Greg's living situation. He visited our home and Greg's school. At the school, he interviewed Greg. I wish I could have been a fly on the wall for that conversation. I can imagine the court representative asking him an important question and getting either no answer or an off-the-wall response about Christmas, *Sesame Street* or something else on Greg's mind.

Overall, the guardianship process took about two months, and went without a hitch until the last day – the day of the court hearing. Greg is rarely sick, but the flu bug hit him that morning. We didn't know that until we were in the hearing room. Just when the magistrate started the hearing, Greg turned to me and said, "Spit." That's the word he uses for vomiting. I hustled him off to the restroom. The magistrate was kind and understanding. She paused the hearing for the ten minutes we needed. By the end of the morning, we were Greg's co-guardians.

Supplemental Security Income (SSI)

The federal government has a means-tested program that provides a monthly benefit for people who are disabled. It's called Supplemental Security Income or SSI. This program is administered by the Social Security Administration. It's funded by general tax revenues, not the social security (FICA) tax.

SSI is available for a minor child with a disability, but the family's resources will be taken into account to determine eligibility. Once the child reaches age 18, the family's resources are no longer considered. At this point, eligibility is based solely on the adult child's resources and earning potential.

We had established a bank account for Greg. We deposited the money he had received in birthday cards and the like. As we approached the SSI process after his 18th birthday, we learned that it was time to make him poor in order to qualify. Considering SSI and Medicaid eligibility requirements, he can't have more than $1,500 in the bank.

The SSI process was smooth for us. Armed with a lot of documentation, we took Greg to our local Social Security Administration office, where they did a face-to-face interview. Within a month, he was approved for SSI and received his first check.

An SSI recipient can have a paying job. The rules are complicated. In general, SSI is reduced by $1 for every $2 earned at a job. Unfortunately, there's no "saving up" of the monthly SSI benefit. Greg still can't have more than $1,500 in the bank. We had to inform well-intentioned benefactors, like grandparents or other family members, that a gift or inheritance could disqualify him from SSI benefits.

Special Needs Trust

Since an SSI recipient can't have many assets, naming Greg in our will or as a life insurance beneficiary could disqualify him from future government benefits. Fortunately, there's a device to address this called a special needs trust. Under a special needs trust, you can leave money for your child with restrictions. The trust is set up to ensure that the child will be eligible for government benefits. Under the trust, the money that you give or leave to the child is spent on things not considered essential, rather to improve the quality of life.

We consulted with a friend who is the parent of an adult with special needs, and an attorney who specializes in this area. He updated our wills and our estate plans, including a special needs trust. When reviewing the estate plans, we came to realize that Greg's sister Anne was key to our future planning. She's mature for her young age. She knows Greg better than anyone outside of our family.

We had open, honest and direct discussions with Anne, going through a lot of "What ifs." We let her know that we appreciated her opinions; that we needed her opinions. We stressed that she didn't have to feel obliged to be Greg's caretaker if we were gone. We educated her about the government benefits that Greg has, or could receive in the future. We let her know about our family's resources and the estate plan. Anne gave us valuable input for Greg's transition planning.

Medicaid Waivers

Unlike guardianships and SSI, Medicaid waivers are not tied to the person reaching the age of majority. The topic of Medicaid waivers is complicated, and subject to change. Anyone who enters the disability world comes to understand the term "waiver." It's a noun, a positive one. It's also a keyword for a tremendously complicated patchwork of government-sponsored services.

The explanation of a waiver starts with Medicaid. Medicaid is a program for health-related services provided to low-income adults and their children, and people with certain disabilities. The federal and state governments jointly fund Medicaid. Each state administers its own program.

In the 1970s, the U.S. special education laws were changing. Education programs became individualized. Segregation was banned, as the phrase "least restrictive environment" became a requirement in the placement of a student with special needs. On a parallel path, in 1981, Medicaid introduced the Home and Community Based Services (HCBS) waiver program to help older adults and people with disabilities live in the least restrictive setting possible. The purpose is to discourage institutionalization, to encourage inclusion of adults with disabilities in the general community.

Ohio has two types of Medicaid waivers. One is called the Level One waiver and it's relatively new. It's designed for individuals with less extensive needs and has a combined benefit limit of $5,000 per year for homemaker, personal care and respite services. Additional Level One funding is also available for other services. In 2009, the average amount paid on behalf of a Level One waiver recipient was almost $9,000.

Ohio's other Medicaid waiver is called the Individual Options or I/O waiver. The I/O waiver has been in use since the early 1990s. I/O waiver funding is, for all practical purposes, unlimited. In 2009, the average amount paid on behalf of an I/O waiver recipient was more than $55,000. This waiver is sometimes used to fund ABA therapy for children with ASD. In Ohio, Medicaid waivers don't technically cover ABA therapy. To get around this, it's paid for under the category of personal or homemaker services.

Greg has a Level One waiver. During his school years, the waiver funded his respite camps at Recreation Unlimited. We knew that the waiver would begin to have even more importance after his transition. We're fortunate to have this waiver, because there are nearly 13,000 people on Ohio's Level One waiting list. On the other hand, Greg is one of more than 25,000 people on Ohio's I/O waiver waiting list. That's a big issue for our long-term planning.

Having taken care of the four early transition steps, we felt well prepared going into Greg's final school year at Project Search.

Chapter 15: A Darn Good Intern

Greg participated in the Project Search program for his final year of school eligibility. He was an intern at the local hospital. With a fabulous teacher, great job coaches and a supportive employer, Greg flourished and grew in that last school year.

His first nine-week assignment was called outtakes. He worked in a medical supply room, going from shelf to shelf, looking for items that were near or past their expiration date. It took a while for Greg to overcome some issues on this new job. The supply room had a loading dock. Whenever a truck was parked in the dock, an overhead light would flash continuously for worker awareness and safety. Greg's peripheral vision is strong, so the flashing light was distracting to him. With the support of his job coach and co-workers, he adapted to this new environment.

Once he got the hang of it, Greg completed the inventory outtakes quickly. His strengths of focus and attention to detail were on display. He did the job faster than regular hospital staff. His accuracy was 100%. Since he'd finished early, they moved him to the surgical supply room, again to do outtakes. Here, he donned a surgery suit and head cover – they called it his "bunny suit." He also finished that job quickly and accurately. There were still a couple of weeks left in the job rotation. A typical worker might have paced himself so that the job lasted for the allotted time. Greg had no idea about milking the time clock.

To fill his time for the rest of the rotation, Greg received a janitorial assignment. He spent the next several weeks mopping the aisles in the hospital. All of them. All four floors. They gave him a spray cleaner bottle. Taught him to spray a four-foot square and then mop it. Then spray another square and mop it. All of the aisles on every floor.

He had a few problems during his mopping days. There was foot traffic in the aisles as he worked. He clipped someone's ankle with his mop once. He also approached a hospital volunteer and lifted the mop toward her face. He was trying, with his limited communication skill, to find out if the mop was dirty and needed changed. Unfortunately, the volunteer had nothing to do with Greg's work.

When I heard about these incidents, I complained to Doreen, "What do they expect? He doesn't have good awareness of people around him, and he has trouble reading social situations." I eventually found out that there was a method to his teacher's madness. She was trying to stretch him – using the mopping job to see if he could navigate around the entire hospital by himself. For her, the negative incidents weren't showstoppers, they were learning opportunities. She eliminated further ankle injuries by teaching Greg to keep to one side of the aisle as he worked, letting others pass by.

The next job in Greg's rotation: Stocking nurse's carts. He used his new navigation skills. He went from hospital room to hospital room with his own cart of supplies, replenishing the nurse's cart in each room. When his own cart ran low on supplies, he would go to an area that housed a computerized central stocking machine. He activated the machine with his fingerprint, and then typed in the codes for the supplies. The machine would dispense them based on the codes that Greg entered. He learned to consult a list of supplies to find the correct code.

One morning at home, Greg had a nick on the forefinger of his right hand, so Doreen put a bandage on it. Later that day, Greg needed to restock his cart from the central stocking machine. A nurse happened by and saw Greg sitting at a break area table near the machine. Incredibly, he appeared to be staging a sit-down strike. He had stopped working!

The nurse called Greg's teacher and job coach. They investigated, learned that the bandage prevented him from getting access to the stocking machine. It couldn't read his fingerprint. Since the machine was "broken," Greg was stumped. So he just sat down. This was another learning opportunity for him. Understanding how to find help from the right person when unexpected things come up.

His final assignment was stocking nurse's carts in the

pre-op and post-op rooms. Here again, his teacher was raising the ante. The pre-op and post-op areas are a much more dynamic environment, compared to the general hospital rooms. They're faster paced, more unpredictable. She wanted to see how Greg would cope with that kind of work environment. He did fine.

His year as a hospital intern was a great success. He far exceeded our expectations. Our best-case scenario was that he'd be able to do some filing or data entry in a controlled office environment. Instead, he practically achieved full independence. By the end of the year, he'd step off the bus in the morning, enter the hospital through a card-access employee area and report to his job site – entirely on his own. His assignments eventually required him to navigate the entire hospital. I would never have imagined that positive outcome.

When the year at Project Search ended, Greg participated in his second graduation ceremony. This time, he'd receive his diploma.

The contrasts with his first graduation a year earlier were many. His social graduation occurred in a sports arena with more than 300 graduates. The Project Search ceremony was in the hospital's large conference room with nine graduating interns. They had worked in many areas of the hospital during the year. At the graduation ceremony, each hospital department that had hosted an intern sent multiple representatives to the ceremony.

Another difference was the display of teamwork. All of the interns had some disability. ASD, Down Syndrome, a traumatic brain injury, etc. Their social skills varied. Greg was probably the least socially adept. As the nine of them sat together in the front of the conference room for the ceremony, you could see a real camaraderie among them. My parents, who attended the ceremony, remarked about this. No competition, no politics, no pretension. The interns looked after each other. If one of the group wasn't sure what to do as the ceremony progressed, the others would immediately offer help and support.

The ceremony included several short presentations. The teacher highlighted each student's personality and accomplishments. She praised Greg for being good with numbers and for his accuracy.

The students got a chance to share their own inspirational message. Most of them came up with something original and personally meaningful. Greg's expressive language deficit made that impossible. Instead, the teacher found an excerpt from Dr. Seuss's *Oh, The Places You'll Go*. She projected the words onto the screen in the conference room for Greg to read aloud:

> *You have brains in your head*
> *You have feet in your shoes*
> *You can steer yourself*
> *Any direction you choose*
> *You're on your own*
> *And you know*

What you know
And you are the guy who'll decide where to go

Greg's rendition was barely audible, and his speaking style is monotonic and fast. This was still a perfect fit. He has scores of Dr. Seuss books. And he's got the capabilities referenced in this passage.

Toward the end of the program, the superintendent from the technical school said a few words. He was nearing retirement, and he was proud of the first year of this new program. He explained how his staff had approached him 18 months earlier with a request: We have to do more for young adults with disabilities who are at the end of their schooling. With the help of the partnering districts and the hospital, the program came together quickly.

Next came the emotional part of the superintendent's remarks. He said when he grew up in the 1950s and 60s, a childhood friend of his had a sister who was developmentally disabled. His voice cracking, he said, "She should have had this available to her." He closed his comments by saying that the graduates of the regular high schools and technical schools "could learn many good lessons from these students." Amen to that.

There was a reception after the graduation. I came upon our school district's transition coordinator and said to her, "You must be happy with this first year's result." She told me about my son's legacy.

She said that Greg's name had come up quite often in the administration's meetings. They had viewed placing him in the Project Search program as a risk. He could follow instructions, but his social and communication weaknesses were a concern. He had decent job skills, but they wondered if he could work independently. They took a chance on him. The result: His performance as an intern was a pleasant surprise.

Because of Greg, the staff was revisiting the capabilities of other students in the system. The meeting discussions went like this: "Let's not sell them short. Look at Greg. We were skeptical about his chances for success, but he hit a home run. We should give some of these other students a chance to show us what they can do." That's a powerful legacy.

The fairy tale ending would be that Greg got full-time paid employment at the hospital, worked there for many years, and became known as the fastest and most accurate stocker in the hospital. That ending was not to be. Greg wasn't offered a position. This wasn't the hospital's fault or his fault.

So as the school year wound down, we started to hunt him up a job.

Chapter 16: Finding Work

In the words of Alice Cooper, "School's out forever." For Greg, it was great while it lasted. He went into his first year of special ed preschool a quiet, unsure little guy. The early years were a great trial for school staff and family. We survived this period of aggression, defiance and destructiveness. He settled into middle school, then high school. His personality became more clear, his strengths more evident. His skills grew beyond our expectations.

As we began the job search, we considered some basic questions: What does he want to do? What makes him happy? The reality is that the answers to those questions can only be educated guesses on our part. The world is still a strange place for Greg. His communication deficit is still there. He's not able to give us those answers in clear terms. We have to infer the answers on his behalf. We base our inferences on a composite of him – the behavior we observe in his daily life.

He likes to be on the go. Each day, he inquires how many times we'll go "bye bye." The destination doesn't much matter to him. It's all in the going. Even coming along to gas up the car counts as a "bye bye" to him. Running errands is fine. Getting a snack or meal out is even better. He's good at the movies, as long as snacks are provided. Likes the park. Enjoys swimming. He might even enjoy boating and fishing, but he came up short in the Dad department there.

He's a great car traveler. Sits patiently through a two, four or 12-hour trip. Listens to the radio. Watches the scenery pass by. Comments on road signs or other things he sees. He once hopefully called our attention to a road sign advertising adult books and videos. Although this is funny, it's not unusual since he enjoys books and videos. But not that kind! I told him we wouldn't be stopping there.

During trips, he takes advantage of the snack bag. Talks to himself. Gets the giggles over something that he finds funny. He's on the go, and he's content. Fifty years ago, John Steinbeck wrote *Travels with Charley*, telling the story of his driving trip across the United States in the company of his good friend – a dog. I've thought about doing that kind of trip with Greg someday. Maybe when I retire or somehow find a month of free time, I could take a long and leisurely car trip with him. I think he'd enjoy that.

He's a good air traveler, too. That's a little harder to manage. We have to monitor his liquid intake, plan his restroom breaks. It's hard for him to understand that he can't use the restroom on an airplane during takeoff and landing preparations. We found that out the hard way when the pilot came over the intercom to announce, "We'll be taking off just as soon as we can get the passenger out of the restroom." Even playing the "A" card (autism) didn't get us any slack from the airline's rules and the unhappy looks from some of our fellow passengers.

At home, he has narrow interests. He'll pass time on the internet. He watches some TV. "Watches" is too strong a word. He'll keep an eye on the TV. He's not much interested in the content, except for *Wheel of Fortune* when he waits patiently for the phrase to be revealed. And *Jeopardy!*, when he likes to hum the tune during the final question. Otherwise, at various times of the day, he likes to have the TV tuned to certain programs. Again, not that he's interested in the content. Rather, he can mentally check off a predictable event. *The Doctors*? Check. *Ellen*? Check. Why not? "Rain Man" had *Judge Wapner*.

It's hard to keep him occupied and stimulated at home. He needs structure and variety.

For the last eight years of his schooling, Greg got used to working as a part of his school life. It started on a small scale, an hour or two per day. For that last school year at the hospital, he was a full-time worker for all practical purposes.

Having a workplace gives his life richness. His socialization skills are still weak, so he's not forming relationships with his co-workers. But he is making acquaintances, adding social variety for him. It gives him another sphere in his life.

What did Greg think about his employment opportunities?

We wish we knew. As his final school year ended, we sensed confusion in him. For the past 20 years, he could count on school restarting in August. He knew it wouldn't restart anymore. We told him he'd get a job and go to work, but we didn't have a concrete plan to show him. This created a seriousness in him. When we talked about the next few months, he'd look at us intently, trying to understand. An abstract idea doesn't communicate well to someone with autism. Just like when we moved from Ohio to Alabama, we needed dates, pictures, an address and a supervisor's name to get him comfortable with the transition from school to work.

No matter what route we took to help Greg find a job, this much we knew: This work thing is not like school, where you enroll in a system and receive services for more than a decade. Jobs come and go. It's likely that Greg will need help finding employment many times during his life. He won't be as lucky as George Kramer, who was featured in a *New York Times Magazine* article. Mr. Kramer is a 71-year-old man with autism, who has worked in the same family hardware store in Brooklyn, New York, for the last 58 years!

As we began the job search process, Doreen and I agreed about the kinds of jobs we thought he could succeed at. Data entry, filing and stocking were at the top of the list. Although he mastered the mopping job at the hospital, his teacher told us that he doesn't enjoy janitorial work. How did she know this? Greg didn't tell her, but she observed his demeanor and behavior when doing janitorial tasks.

Doreen and I weren't in total agreement about the ideal work schedule. I pictured Greg working nearly full-time. Six or seven hours per day, four days per week. On the fifth day, I pictured him enrolled in an adult day services program – to give him more of a recreational outlet. Doreen saw him working a few less hours or days, and using adult day services a little more. We were both flexible on this point.

With the help of our case manager and the school district's transition coordinator, we learned about Greg's four basic options for work.

The first is a **sheltered workshop**, where the clients report to the same government-operated work site each day. All of the workers are people with disabilities. In Ohio, each county has an agency that provides services to people with developmental disabilities. These are called County DD Boards, and they operate these workshops. A challenge for these sites is to have enough meaningful work to keep the clients occupied. One of the saddest outcomes is when the task is reduced to "make work." The worst example of this is when the workers assemble and then disassemble the same item throughout the day. No way to feel productive in that kind of work environment.

There are many positive stories about sheltered workshops. With dedicated staff, the workshops become a community, a family. My employer, Honda, has contracted with a sheltered workshop in Ohio for more than 20 years. The workers assemble owner's manual kits for every Honda vehicle made in Ohio, Canada and Indiana. This is steady and important work. Every vehicle coming off six different Honda assembly lines needs to have the correct owner's manual kit in the glove box.

In 2010, this county workshop, operating under the name of U-CO Industries, earned recognition for their high quality and on-time delivery to Honda. This is all the more impressive when you understand the criteria for this recognition are the same for U-CO as they are for private, for-profit auto parts suppliers.

The second work option is an **enclave environment**. The county DD board provides a workforce of individuals with disabilities and a supervisory presence at an employer's location in the community. The clients work together as a team, taking care of a function at the sponsoring employer's business. The number of enclave opportunities depends on the number of local businesses who are willing to be sponsors. General economic conditions affect these work sites.

The third option is **community supported employment**. In Ohio, state government agencies provide support services to help people with disabilities find a competitive job in the community. The search is sometimes called "job development." The object is to match the client's skills to an employer's needs. This is done by working with existing job openings or having a job developer work with an employer to "carve out" a job. Instead of an existing position, a group of functions that align with the client's skills become a made-to-order job. If a match is found, job coaching is made available for a short period. After that, the client is expected to function on his or her own, like a regular employee at that business or organization.

The last option is **do-it-yourself**. Find a job on your own. If your community is like mine, you see people with disabilities performing retail jobs. Grocery store baggers, movie theater ticket takers. My childhood friend's son, who has Asperger's, has a steady job at a big box retailer. One of his main duties is shopping cart control.

As Greg's year as a hospital intern was ending, we began the community supported employment process. He was assigned a job developer who began to search for a job that matched Greg's skills. This didn't yield any immediate results, so, on a parallel path, we took on the do-it-yourself option. A friend provided us with a lead for an organization that potentially had office work available. We followed up. By the time Greg graduated from Project Search, that referral became our one and only job option for him.

Greg's first paying job is at the Association for the Developmentally Disabled (ADD) in Columbus, Ohio. ADD is a not-for-profit organization established in the 1970s. They provide adult day services, operate residential facilities, and provide caregivers. A few years ago, they started the vocational program where Greg now works.

He works in an office environment. The employees digitize paper records using a scanner and computer. There's a copy center where the workers prepare binders. They print, fold and mail brochures. There's a data entry function. For one data entry task, employees enter the weekly time and attendance data for ADD's entire workforce.

This work fits Greg to a tee. His new work environment is comfortable for him and us. We've found that it's best to go with your gut feeling. When we visited the ADD worksite, it felt good for Greg. We had a positive connection with the management and staff. The company has been in operation for 40 years, and that appealed to us. There's a 6-to-1 staff ratio, so any support he needs for his job is nearby.

He's a part-time employee, working five hours a day, three days a week, at Ohio's minimum wage of $7.40 per hour. Greg's Medicaid waiver covers the cost of transportation – he's picked up and dropped off in our driveway.

The supervisory staff is impressed with his accuracy and his fine motor skills. He alphabetizes to several levels. First by county, then by month and last name. He's found a niche as the tri-fold brochure specialist. Greg's a perfectionist, and the brochures are folded perfectly straight.

Three months into his new job, we received a positive written report about Greg's performance:

> *We assigned Greg the task of data entry on a project of returned forms which required not only accurate keying, spelling and word placement, but also discerning the documents to capture forms which had approvals and*

> *which did not. Greg exhibited amazing accuracy, got the Excel spreadsheet done very quickly, and nothing needed corrected. Wonderful job!*

When work is not feasible or available, adults with ASD can receive adult day services. In our community, private companies, both for-profit and not-for-profit, operate these programs. These programs are also called adult day care or "dayhabs."

There are many options for adult day services. They vary in size; some serving as few as ten adults, others serving 40 or more. They are available in urban and rural settings. The programs we observed have a recreational component. Community outings are available every week. Some of the programs have a vocational component on site.

The main difference between the school setting and adult day services lies in the premise. In school, there is learning activity guided by an IEP. Goals are established, progress is measured and reported. In adult day services, growth and progress are not necessarily expected. Some programs do try to track individual progress, formally or informally.

During our day program research for Greg, we visited a brand new facility that was just about to open. We talked to the owner and asked why she had decided to go into the business. She explained that she had a brother with special needs who had passed away. She'd taught special education in a nearby school district for many years. She worked hard to help her students, who were of high school age. She found that many of those students stayed home, doing nothing, after their education years ended. This broke her heart. She decided to do something about it by getting into the adult day services business. Her husband and son were also part of the business. They continue to honor her brother's memory.

A positive aspect of adult day services is community. Friendships and bonds are formed among the participants. Adults with ASD may not seek or crave social interaction. The structure and stimulus provided by adult day services is helpful.

Greg's job is part-time, three days a week – Tuesday through Thursday. We wanted to fill the other two days with an adult day services program. After doing our research, we narrowed the list to three programs. We visited each one. The program we chose is called Dreamshine. It's in a rural setting, relatively small, serving less than 20 adults each day. Again, we went with our gut. Ten minutes into our visit, Anne remarked, "I can see Greg here."

Besides the small size, another plus for us was Dreamshine's focus on occupational skills. Participants tend to gardens on site. They have a small candle-making business. There's the possibility of Greg doing some office work. It's a supportive environment where he'll get individualized attention. His Medicaid waiver is very helpful here, covering the cost of the program and transportation.

A few months after he began to participate in the adult day services program, Dreamshine had a family open house on a Saturday morning. We attended with Greg and his grandparents. In talking with the staff that morning, we sensed that they had come to know him well. Greg had formed positive bonds with his new Monday/Friday family.

Although the initial arrangements for work and adult day services are going well, there's a gap between Greg's hospital intern experience and his first paying job. At the hospital, he was working independently, included in a regular community setting. His co-workers were people without disabilities. His paying job at ADD is a much more sheltered environment. We feel a bit guilty that his capabilities are underutilized.

His Project Search teacher is disappointed. I can't blame her. She and her staff put in a lot of time and effort to stretch Greg's capabilities. She hoped he'd get a job within the hospital's system, or a similar job at another employer. She believes in Greg. Wants him fully included in the adult working world, pulling his own weight and using his strengths.

Two factors explain our decision. First, it was the only job available when Greg graduated – a bird in the hand. We didn't want Greg in adult day services five days a week. We wanted him to begin to understand year-round work.

Secondly, even though the scope of the job is more limited than his intern experience, it seems like a comfortable place for him. In addition, the organization provides transportation services, relieving Doreen of nearly two hours of driving on each of his workdays.

We're not giving up. We're still in just the first year of his post-school life. In the future, we can consider other work opportunities for him. In fact, he just started going back to the hospital as a volunteer. He goes once a week for an hour, and does the same nurse's cart stocking job he did as an intern.

When we step back and take stock, we can say that he's made the initial transition smoothly. The most important thing for him is having a set schedule – this makes his life predictable. It's important to keep him occupied and stimulated. He seems happy with his new working life, continuing to grow his capabilities and impress us. I know he's got more upside potential.

Earlier in this chapter, I mentioned that as Greg's final school year as a hospital intern wound down, we sensed confusion in him. He showed a seriousness trying to understand his own future. Now that the school-to-work transition is complete, he can explain it very well – in his own way. In fact, he and I had a recent conversation on this topic. During that conversation, he inadvertently provided the title of this book.

We were talking about the latter part of his school history. I provided the commentary: "August 2007, Dublin Jerome High School. August 2008, Power Plus. August 2009, Project Search. August 2010, no more school. School is done." At this point, he joined the conversation and said, "What happens next? *Sesame Street*, same and different. ADD and Dreamshine."

Let me explain. "Same and different" is one of his common observations. For example, if he sees a Diet Coke commercial on TV, he'll point to the TV and to our refrigerator and say, "Same and different."

He remembers an old *Sesame Street* game show skit entitled, "What Happens Next?" In the skit, Gordon presents a situation and asks the audience to predict what will happen. Greg applied the game show's idea to his state of mind at the time school was ending. Then he answered the question by naming his workplace (ADD) and adult day services program (Dreamshine).

What happens next? Don't we all want to know that?

Chapter 17: A Housing Dilemma

Returning to Ms. Kingsley's essay about that trip to Holland. She wrote, "But everyone you know is busy coming and going from Italy, and they're all bragging about what a wonderful time they had there." Maybe that refers to the jealousy felt by the parent of a child with special needs, wishing that you had the life of a "normal" parent. That notion hasn't been in our minds so much – until recently.

Under normal circumstances, our active parenting days would be winding down. Our two kids in their early twenties would be on their own – or at least moving in that direction. We see that in our circle of family and friends. With kids out of the house, the couples are experiencing new freedom. They're able to pick up and go on short notice. We're not in that place. Since Greg can't be left alone, our choices are to get a caregiver or bring him along.

This brings a sharp focus to the question, "What are we going to do with him?" We're a long way from sorting that out. It involves both our heads and our hearts.

Our heads say the clock is ticking. We hope to have 20 or 30 more years on this earth, while Greg could have more than 50. He's familiar and comfortable with his current living arrangements. We worry that we may be doing him a long-term disservice by the degree of flexibility and spontaneity he has. We know that if and when we move him out of our house, it will take some time for him to adjust. It would be better to introduce him to a new housing arrangement when he's in his 20s, as opposed to his 60s. Our heads also say that we're financially responsible for his future. He doesn't yet have access to a level of government support that provides full-time caregivers.

Our hearts are the source of that empty nest jealousy. When he's away at the overnight respite camp, we enjoy the quiet in our house and freedom to do as the mood strikes. On the other hand, we've invested 100,000 hours raising him. His birth made us a family in the first place. We don't look forward to leaving him at his own house or apartment. That'll be much more difficult than dropping off Anne at college.

The truth is that Greg can't live on his own. Excerpts from the last several years of his evaluations and assessments:

> *Greg was administered the Reynolds Intellectual Assessment Scale. His scores were in the extremely low range for verbal and non-verbal intelligence, and in the average range for nonverbal memory.*

Greg's Conceptual standard scores were in the extremely low range of functioning.

Greg's Social standard scores were in the lower extreme range. The social skills area was Greg's most significant area of weakness.

Greg's Practical standard scores were in the extremely low range; however, ratings indicate he demonstrates strengths in school living and self-care.

Greg's reading, writing and math skills are significantly below what is expected given his age.

Greg is reading Level 4, Book 6. This is 2.5 grade level.

He is a fluent reader, but demonstrates little comprehension.

Greg is unable to monitor his own medical well-being.

Greg needs a high level of support for demonstrating correct safety procedures in emergency situations.

Greg has no telephone skills and is unable to handle emergencies independently.

Greg is able to count money, identify coins and bills, and understand that money is used to purchase goods, but has no concept of the value of money.

Greg struggles to carry on a two way conversation.

Greg uses little inflection and few changes in his volume of speech.

> *When Greg's initial attempts at seeking information or assistance are unsuccessful because he has not been complete or specific enough, he does not demonstrate means for making repairs to make his intent more clear. He tends to repeat his original communication over and over rather than make changes that will allow his listener to better understand the intent of his communication.*
>
> *It is difficult to determine how much information Greg attends to and how he feels about being a part of a group. Greg is respectful and genuine with those he interacts with.*
>
> *Greg often looks for reassurance when completing tasks.*
>
> *Greg does not seek or develop personal goals; however, he demonstrates happiness with particular tasks. When completing these tasks, he is quiet, attentive and accurate.*
>
> *His teachers indicated that Greg is compliant, has great penmanship, and loves numbers.*
>
> *Greg presents with a very strong foundation of fine motor skills. Cursive and print are performed extremely diligently with exact information, sizing and spacing. Greg is intolerant of errors and will erase and edit his writing repeatedly to ensure accuracy.*

It's hard to read about your adult child in these stark terms. They make it clear that Greg can't live independently.

We're only beginning to explore residential options for Greg. Aside from keeping him at home with us, there are three options.

One option is institutionalization. This was the solution 60 years ago. State-run institutions still exist, but in much smaller numbers. There are ten large institutions, called developmental centers, in Ohio. There's general agreement among the government, disability advocates and families: this is a last resort option. However, these institutions represent important options for developmentally disabled adults. They provide crisis management, temporary placements and placement for criminal offenders with developmental disabilities.

The second option is an ICFMR. These are Intermediate Care Facilities for the Mentally Retarded. (This name should be changed – to get rid of the R-word.) These are medium sized residential facilities. Although they might technically be considered institutions, they're generally smaller and spread throughout the community. Approximately 7,500 adults with disabilities live in ICFMRs in Ohio. We've visited a few in our town. One was a second floor of a warehouse-type building. It had dormitory-style rooms, common bathrooms, a community kitchen and family room. Another was a single story apartment complex. The buildings were converted into pods for six people each. Again, the kitchen and family room areas were common. The ICFMRs are staffed 24/7. Clients are transported to jobs or adult day programs, and return to the facility for the evening.

Here, I'd also list a subcategory called specialized ICFMRs. This is my own term, meant to describe a facility where all of the clients live and work. These are rare, but we've seen a couple of them in our travels. One is Bittersweet Farms in

Northwest Ohio. This facility has been around since 1983. Their model is exclusively for people with autism, a 24/7 farm community for living and working. They currently have 20 full-time residents, which is the maximum they're permitted to have. There are a handful of similar facilities across the country. A new facility, called Safe Haven Farms, recently opened in the Cincinnati, Ohio, area.

Another specialized ICFMR is Rainbow Omega in Eastaboga, Alabama. This residential facility opened in 1995 and serves about 80 clients in a number of housing units on the same site. They also have a greenhouse and an occupational center where clients work. The occupational center is where Rainbow Omega assembles the owner's manual kits for Honda's auto plant in Alabama.

The third option is a house or apartment in the community. This has been the recent trend. We're fortunate to live in an area with a very active residential program for people with disabilities. An organization called Creative Housing has made hundreds of living places available, at discounted rents, throughout the greater Columbus, Ohio, community.

In this living arrangement, staffing is handled separately. The staffing solution doesn't come with the apartment or house. That presents a management challenge to schedule and coordinate caregivers. It can also become an insurmountable financial barrier that prevents transition from the family home. This leads to the important topic of caregivers for adults.

In the institutional and ICFMR settings, caregiving is included. Staff is on-site 24/7. Transportation is provided, to work or to adult day services. These are turnkey solutions. This approach comes at a price. First, the cost to taxpayers. In Ohio, the average cost of caring for someone in a developmental center is $123,000 per year. For an ICFMR, the average cost is $83,000 per year. These high costs are a function of both the overhead associated with operating these types of facilities and the concentration of staffing.

There's a different kind of price paid by the residents: less flexibility. Common eating, living and bathroom areas represent less individualization. Without a personal caregiver, the residents have less opportunity for spontaneous outings.

The model for homes or apartments in the community is more individualized. Some residents may need only minimal support. They may be able to be left unattended overnight, needing support only for meal preparation and transportation. Other residents may need support services around the clock for their security and safety. Therefore, in the community setting, each resident makes separate arrangements for the necessary caregiving staff, usually with support from the County DD Board.

We've ruled out institutionalization. In addition, our opinion is that an ICFMR would be too confining for Greg. We've created this problem. We've conditioned him to be out and about. He has one or more outings practically every day – whether running errands, going to the library, getting a snack or a meal.

Our thinking is a home or apartment in the community. We're fortunate to live in a community where there are affordable residential options. The physical residence part seems simple. But he'll need caregivers. That's where it gets difficult financially.

If we move Greg out of our home, he's going to need a lot of oversight. He needs someone with him all of the time. There are 168 hours in a week. Suppose 40 of those hours are occupied with work, adult day services and travel to and from those places. That leaves 128 hours. At a cost of $12-16/hour, more than $75,000 per year. We can do some of the care giving ourselves. We're not immortal; we need to think of how he'll get along without us in the long run.

His current Level One Medicaid waiver provides $5,000 per year for personal care services. He receives a monthly SSI check, which adds up to about $9,000 per year. Currently, he works about 60 hours per month at minimum wage – that's another $5,000 per year, but it reduces his SSI by $2,100 per year. Combining all of his available resources, we're still more than $50,000 short of the annual amount required for caregivers. What's more, he can't save up his own money. Can't put anything away for the future. If his bank account exceeds $1,500, he'll lose his Medicaid waiver and SSI.

It would be hard for us to manage this on Greg's behalf without a more generous waiver. Ohio's I/O waiver would provide that necessary support. He's on the waiting list for that waiver. Sadly, Greg would stand a much better chance of moving to the top of that list if we abandoned him. He'd then be considered an emergency case.

The families of people with ASD all face unique circumstances and decisions. I can understand why some go the ICFMR route. The finances are much simpler. If we elected to place Greg in an ICFMR, he'd simply turn his entire SSI check over to the facility. If he had a job and made money, he'd get to keep only a tiny amount each month – the rest would go to the facility.

The ICFMR is a viable option. Today, we don't think it's right for Greg. Some years from now, we may change our tune. For now, we'll keep him at home, until we find a solution that suits him and us. We won't abandon him.

Chapter 18: What I Want To Say

I'll never be mistaken for Tony Robbins or any other master of inspiration or motivation. I'm just a father with something to say.

The time leading up to Greg's transition from school was stressful. I felt a responsibility to gather the necessary information, to do the right things for him. This was also a period of reflection for me. Two decades of schooling was coming to an end. I kept thinking back, reliving the experience of raising him.

Some people find it helpful for mental health to keep a diary or a journal. I started my own therapy to carry me through Greg's transition planning. I began acquiring and organizing reference material, taking notes and making "to do" lists, keeping myself on track. Had we covered all the bases for Greg? Which applications were pending? What was left to do?

Greg's transition is in process. He's working and receiving adult day services. Doreen and I know that we'll either be providing or directly managing Greg's care for the rest of our lives. We have the tools and the confidence to do that job. We're just a little short in the resources needed to set Greg up in his own place.

Having navigated the initial transition steps, I now have the time and perspective to speak.

The first group I'd reach out to are the parents of younger children with ASD. Doreen and I know the heartbreak of receiving the diagnosis. We know that raising a child with ASD can be all-encompassing. You're not thinking 20 years down the road. Sometimes you wonder if you'll make it through the next 20 hours or 20 minutes. It's important for parents to see the long arc of life for their child with ASD. The parents are – by far – the most capable advocates for that child. To them falls the loving and the caregiving, also the planning for their child's future. These parents should be able to raise their heads and look further down the road. To see a vision of how their child can be included in the community as an adult.

Next, there's the extended families. Grandparents, aunts, uncles, cousins, neighbors and close friends. As the incidence rate of ASD has increased, I've met many people who've told me that their co-worker, neighbor or relative has a child on the spectrum. These extended family members usually aren't on the front lines – they don't live with the person with ASD. But I've found that they want more knowledge about autism. They want to know how to be supportive. These extended family members should think about their loved one holistically. They can lend support, help clear a path that will result in some good benefit in the future of that child. Progress won't be linear for a child with ASD. It's two steps forward and one back. Progress will occur with support and encouragement.

Another group is the education professionals. We're fortunate that our experience with teachers and school administrators was positive. I'm not naïve. I've spoken to parents, teachers and school administrators who are frustrated. I want to reinforce the passion to educate children with autism. The kind of passion I see in my daughter, who is on the verge of entering the field. Buoyed with optimism, unstained by cynicism.

Education has been a front-burner political issue since George Washington was President. Everyone's a stakeholder. Everyone's got an opinion, whether it be about funding, standards or something else. There are a lot of positives in our system of special education. It's much better than 40 years ago, thanks to brave people who fought to end segregated special education in the 1970s. It's up to us to honor their legacy by continuing to improve the educational services for young people with ASD.

On a broader scale, there's the important relationship between the autism community and various professionals. Doctors, researchers, therapists, service providers, politicians, government agency administrators. I've been active in the autism community over the years. I have some experience. I was the President of the Central Ohio

Chapter of the Autism Society of America. I served on the board of the state autism societies in Ohio and Alabama, and on a County DD Board in Ohio. I was a member of the Ohio Governor's Autism Task Force. I learned a lot from these experiences. There are great people working to make things better for people with ASD. There's also too much bureaucracy and red tape.

Autism awareness is at an all-time high. Research is progressing. We have good momentum. We must continue to push for early diagnosis and early intervention. Yet, I can't help but think that we've got a blind spot: adults with ASD. To be sure, there are people who are actively working on transition and adult services. There are also some organizations focused on this issue. For example, there's a non-profit consortium called Advancing Futures for Adults with Autism. Even so, I don't feel that there is enough intensity to address the issue of services for adults with ASD.

The increased incidence rate for ASD is going to put further pressure on an already strained home and community based services system. In Ohio, the I/O waiver is the holy grail for families with disabilities. Is it sustainable? Other states have studied or implemented autism-specific waivers. What assumptions have they made about the incidence rate and the services that will be required for adults? Some school-age children with ASD are waiver recipients, and are accessing waiver funds for ABA and other services. Can the same waiver programs grow in order to continue to support school-age children as well as the growing number of adults? What's a reasonable number of people to be on a waiting list?

What's a reasonable waiting time?

As our country recovers from the recession, federal, state and local governments face very tough times. Special education, adult services and Medicaid might not be immune from the budget ax. This is a recipe for big trouble – a growing population that needs to receive services from a shrinking resource pool. It's time for the autism community to join with a wide range of professionals to shed some light on the topic of adult services. Autism is, after all, a lifelong neurological disorder.

People with ASD have a lot to offer. They are some of the most interesting people walking this earth. They have many talents that can be put to good use in our society. We need a comprehensive approach to support people with ASD. Access to evidence-based therapies such as ABA for children is a good thing. It's not the end-all. Let's get a realistic estimate of the resources required to support all children and adults with ASD. Then let's set about to find and deploy those resources.

Next, to those I know the best. Doreen, you've done three times the amount of work that should be expected of any mother. You helped Greg with every single step of his progress, and you hung in there all the times when he regressed. In the last four years, when my job took me out of town, you've taken the full burden on your shoulders. Setting all of that aside, your biggest contribution is the true essence of motherhood, the uncanny intuition that tells you what needs to be done, and how it needs to be done. It's why some things have always been non-negotiable for you. Because you're the Mom. You've got Greg's back, and he knows it.

Anne, I know we've saved more of Greg's artwork and projects. But let's be honest, he's a much better artist. God may have thrown us a curveball with Greg's autism. But he also sent us a secret weapon – you. I can't imagine raising Greg without you. Now, you're setting out to help lots of people like him. I'm not sure where you'll go with your career, but I know I'll enjoy watching it.

Finally, to Greg. You can't speak for yourself – not in ways that most people could understand. You've learned how to function in all kinds of work and social environments. You're a keen observer of this world that you've been put in. You've made a lasting impression on the people who've come to know you. For all those accomplishments and more, you deserve to be recognized. And you're not done. You have a whole adult lifetime in front of you. I know that you'll continue to shine.

I love you, Greg, just the way you are.

Appendix

Medicaid Waiver Background Information

The Centers for Medicaid Services website explains that Section 1915(c) of the Social Security Act covers HCBS Waivers, and it provides the Health and Human Services Secretary authority "to waive Medicaid provisions in order to allow long-term care services to be delivered in community settings. This program is the Medicaid alternative to providing comprehensive long-term services in institutional settings." In other words, the standard of care for people with disabilities remains institutionalization, but the waiver programs are vehicles to access care in alternative community settings.

It took me a good long while to understand the meaning of the term waiver. I wondered what the recipient would be "waiving" or giving up, in order to receive the services. The answer is basically nothing, other than institutionalization. The name "waiver" comes from the fact that, under these programs, the federal government agrees not to apply some bureaucratic requirements to the state.

Let's look at the number of people being served by these waivers. First, a caveat. The data listed below is not all concurrent. The oldest data referenced below is from 2005. The newest is from 2009.

In 2005, across the 50 states, there were 433,000 people participating in waiver programs targeted for people with developmental disabilities. That year, these people received services valued at $17 billion, for an average of $39,000 per participant. By the 2008 government fiscal year, the value of these waiver services had grown to $21.7 billion.

Ohio currently has two waiver programs for people with developmental disabilities. The data below is for 2009, except for the waiting list information, which is 2007.

	Individual Options (I/O)	**Level One**	**Total**
No. of Participants	15,406	7,101	22,507
Value of Waiver Services	**$850.5 million**	**$63.2 million**	**$913.7 million**
Amount per Participant	**$55,200**	**$8,900**	**$40,600**
No. of People on Waiting List	25,370	12,743	38,113

The Level One waiver is relatively new. It is designed for individuals with less extensive needs and has a combined benefit limit of $5,000 per year for homemaker, personal care, transportation and respite services. Additional Level

One funding is also available for other services.

Ohio's I/O waiver has been around a lot longer, since the early 1990s. Participants are slotted into funding ranges, based on their needs. But there is currently no limit or cap on an individual's I/O funding. In Ohio's current program, the requirement for the I/O waiver is that the average cost of benefits per enrollee cannot exceed the average cost of serving an individual in an ICFMR. For reference, in 2005, the cost per person in an Ohio ICFMR was $82,900. So the 2009 I/O waiver cost per person of $55,200 meets Ohio's requirement to be below the ICFMR cost. This is part of the ultimate rationale for the waivers: People with disabilities living in less restrictive settings that are more cost-efficient.

Waiting lists are an issue in Ohio. For every person receiving waiver services, there are 1.8 people waiting. The criteria for entrance to Ohio's I/O waiver include:

- *individuals who receive adult services and reside in their own home or their family's home and intend to remain there*
- *individuals whose primary caregiver is age 60 or older*
- *individuals under age 22 whose needs are unusual in scope or intensity*

There are also provisions for granting an I/O waiver on an emergency basis.

Waiver funding is a partnership between the federal and state governments. The federal government provides 60% of the funding. The states provide the other 40%.

Notes and Citations

Chapter 1, page 15-16
Welcome to Holland ©1987 by Emily Perl Kingsley. All rights reserved. Reprinted by permission of the author.

Chapter 7, page 55
"Parents of kids with autism not more likely to get divorced, study says," May 19, 2010, Madison Park (cnn.com)

Chapter 11, page 112
"Family to Receive $1.5M+ in First-Ever Vaccine-Autism Court Award," September 9, 2010, Sharyl Attkisson (cbsnews.com)

Chapter 11, page 113
"This Question Has Been Asked and Answered," January 16, 2009, Claudia Kalb interview of Allison Singer (newsweek.com)

Chapter 15, page 139-140
Oh, The Places You'll Go ©1960 by Dr. Seuss Enterprises, L.P.

Chapter 16, page 146
"What About George," January 10, 2010, Saki Knafo, *New York Times Magazine*

Chapter 17, page 161
"Disability in Ohio: Managing the Projected Need for Long-Term Supports," January 2010, Shahla Mehdizadeh, Scripps Gerontology Center, Miami University

Appendix
"Medicaid HCBS Waiver Expenditures FY 2003 Through FY 2008 - Table 4 Developmental Disabilities Waivers," November 30, 2009 (hcbs.org)

Fiscal Plan for Home and Community-Based Waiver Services, December 31, 2009, Ohio Department of Developmental Disabilities

State of Ohio MRDD Futures Committee Final Report, March 28, 2008

Acknowledgments

I first want to thank my dear cousin Christa Sidman, who read my initial jumble of words and gave me professional advice. Most importantly, Christa encouraged me to continue with the project. I'd have never finished without her vote of confidence.

Thanks to Doreen and Anne, who helped me remember the stories and gave me tons of support.

Thanks also to Anne's roomies at OSU, most of whom had the misfortune to have me as the coach of their elementary school basketball team. Now, as worldly college grads, they keep me connected to the younger generation. I was motivated by their positive comments. Thanks especially to Jessica – a great writer whose opinion I value.

Huge thanks to my friend Don Penny, who contributed substantial edits and advice. Don's talent and insight are amazing. You too, Susan.

Thanks to o2ideas in Birmingham. Their creative abilities helped bring everything together. Thanks especially to Bill, Roger, Ellen and Joey. And, of course, Shelley Stewart a.k.a. The Godfather. I'm honored to count him among my friends.

Finally, thanks to our extended families. Their support has been critical in raising Greg. We've never felt like we were going it alone. A special shout out to Mom and Dad. Your enduring devotion to your grandson has made a world of difference.